ADVANC

"A transformation in education is unfolding, and this book is a must-read for those individuals who wish to be a part of catalyzing positive change and have access to the latest information on ground-breaking research and practical strategies for cultivating an educational system in which administrators, teachers, and all students can flourish and succeed.

"Through engaging dialogue, stories, and inspiring quotes, the authors have assembled a rich and compelling volume that integrates not only the 'why' of educational reform, but the 'how.' I highly recommend this book for courses in teacher preparation, graduate courses in education as well as practitioners who wish to join the 'call' for creating an educational system in which teachers and their students can learn and thrive."

*Kimberly A. Schonert-Reichl, Ph.D., Professor University of British Columbia*

"This book delivers fully on its promise of providing 'a pathway to enlivening and transforming education' through the authors' experiences, insights, and clarity of ideas and representative anecdotes and strategies. They achieve their goal of guiding the reader to consider the whole child through engagement, inquiry, personalization, and emotional connections. Teachers receive tools to be detectives looking for the unique gifts and potentials in all children and how to best nourish them to fruition."

*Judy Willis, M.D., M.Ed., Neurologist, Teacher, Grad School Ed faculty, Author*

"A powerful account of the problems facing schools in an era of uncertainty and chaos—and an optimistic pathway for transforming education. Experiential wisdom is blended with the latest research on the brain and deep learning. Inspiring stories and practical strategies are weaved into this map for creating turn-around teachers who draw out the strength and resilience of all students."

*Larry K. Brendtro, PhD. , Founder, Reclaiming Youth International*

"*Unwritten* follows in the historic footsteps of John Dewey's progressive education reform *Democracy and Education* (1916) and Charles Silberman's national bestseller, *Crisis in the Classroom: The Remaking of American Education (1970)*. *Unwritten* integrates all the new concepts of psychological learning and neuroscience. It is a must-read book for anyone who believes that significant and lifelong learning is based on relationships and human connections rather than standardized content and computer programs."

*Nicholas J. Long Ph.D., Professor Emeritus, American University, President of the Life Space Crisis Intervention Institute*

"*Unwritten* is the story of What Could Be in American Education. Founded in the beliefs that *programs do not change people; people change people* and that real *learning is profoundly relational*.

"*Unwritten* guides readers to understand schools as living systems and to envision them as nurturing entities that cultivate caring connections between adults and students and nurture the strengths and abilities of the young people they serve. Desautels and McKnight draw upon human development, neuroscience, and trauma-informed principles to offer strategies and suggestions for how schools can reach and teach students, including the troubled and troubling children whose alienation our current system too often perpetuates."

*Signe Whitson, LSW, CEO of the Life Space Crisis Intervention (LSCI) Institute*

"Desautels and McKnight are pioneers by bringing practical strategies for a needed pendulum swing in education that celebrates and honors educators and their ability to cultivate the unique gifts of every child. This is a powerful, thought provoking and refreshing read!"

*Christopher H. Kobik, Teacher, Principal, Superintendent*

"For anyone who cares about learning and maximizing student potential, reading this book will be a jolt of wisdom and inspiration. Desautels and McKnight have identified the crucial elements for establishing authentic connections with students. *Unwritten* provides genuine insights into teaching with the heart and brain in mind.

"It is packed with clear and concise strategies, and a vivid array of stories from the front line that are as instructive as they are entertaining. This book is a terrific resource for educators, parents, and anyone who cares about learning. I enjoyed every page!"

*Terry Small, B.Ed., M.A., Canada's leading Learning Skills Specialist*

"In a world of testing, reform and chaos, Lori and Michael take us to the root of education — relationships — to show us a way out. Not until we focus on the social and emotional well-being of our students will we succeed. *Unwritten* gives teachers, parents and youth workers practical information and easy to use methods to build community that nurtures our children."

*Tim Nation, Executive Director and Cofounder Peace Learning Center*

"Dr. Desautels work with practitioners is transforming to education through her research. The transformation occurs both with educators through the professional development and training outlined in this book and also with the application level in the classroom. Oftentimes there is a disconnect between great learning for an educator and application to a classroom. This book will tie both together for remarkable impact!"

*Dr. Nikki Woodson, Superintendent, Washington Township*

"So many young people are coming into our classrooms anxious, in pain and desperate to be seen and respected. Master teachers know that without relationships, connections and heart, there can be no true learning. Desautels and McKnight have written about this essence of teaching and learning. They have gotten to the core of our educational crisis, and it is not more testing or behavioral battles. It is optimism, belonging and humanity! This book should be required reading for teacher preparation programs. The 'sparks' at the end of each chapter will ignite great collaborative conversations and self-reflection for new and veteran teachers."

*Barbara J. Makoski, M.A., Superintendent of Schools*

"This is a fabulous book for all educators, parents, and governmental bodies for education. This is a book that ties all we are learning about the way the brain learns into a practical format for all to read and understand. It is written in such an easy format that teachers can pick this up and begin to apply what is inside. One of the most powerful statements is 'the story of a living system that knows compassion, that feels the joys and suffering of humankind, but oftentimes, loses its way in an industrial robotic environment where people are unable to thrive.' We often forget in the hurried world of education, meeting the standards and covering the content, that we are teaching students, not teaching the content. As educators we have to remember to allow our students to thrive. This book brings that to life for us."

*Mary Kay Hunt, Director of Instruction and Professional Development, Metropolitan School District of Pike Township*

"Lori and Michael have effectively demonstrated the imperative of personal connections and relationships as high leverage to enhance learning and performance in school. Our current school 'reform' efforts have been largely focused on unpacking standards, formative and summative assessments, and tinkering with school and governance structures, ignoring what brain research tells us about learning and the value of emotional and social development through positive adult relationships.

"These experienced teacher leaders advocate the long needed shift from our current industrial age, deficit-based system toward a system of personalized learning grounded in positive relationships that celebrate student strengths and well-being. Their message is valuable to anyone who would like to experience a better day with their challenging student, understanding why they do what they do, with practical recommendations."

*Mark Stanwood, Ed.D. currently leads the New Jersey School Administrator Residency Program*

"*Unwritten* is a fabulous read! Each page engages the reader with practical tips to use in their classrooms to meet the needs of some of their most challenging students. I found myself underlining many different quotes and ideas that I will use with educators and leaders in my district. Dr. Desautels and Mr. McKnight have confirmed that there are many strategies and tools we can try each and every day to help our students make connections to their learning and gain more from their educational experiences.

"The book is so easy to follow due to the stories and anecdotes Desautels and McKnight include from their own experiences. As a reader and public school educator, I could relate to the children and situations they described throughout the book. It definitely makes me want to go back into the classroom to continue to build the relationships and make connections with all students. I can't wait to put this into the hands of many teachers in my schools, so that they all understand the importance of building these relationships from the start. They will be able to use so many of the tips that will change the dynamic of their rooms. I would encourage all educators to read this great resource to improve the culture and climate of their classrooms and buildings!"

*Kimberly Piper, Director of Elementary Education*
*Metropolitan School District of Washington Township*

"Desautels and McKnight do an excellent job of explaining the urgency of bringing focus to social and emotional systems within the context of educating our at-risk youth. In doing so, they identify research on pain-based behaviors and their relationship to neurobiological systems.

"The book reads as a call to action to reform the current educational 'reform' in America by identifying what is not working and why. The anecdotal stories and scenarios presented throughout the book support the idea of viewing students through a holistic lens, that basic needs must be met in order for them to be effectively educated, and that part of their education must include opportunities to focus on an awareness of our own emotions and behaviors.

"The reader will see disruptive behaviors in a different light, have a better understanding of their causality, and realize the impact that one or two caring individuals can have on a troubled human's life. They will be able to use the 'Sparks' found throughout the book as starting points to begin implementing the many useful concepts found in the text. The book should be required reading for all educators, but would also be useful for the many other professions that require a sense of the human condition."

*J. Kenyon Kummings, Superintendent for Wildwood Public Schools, Wildwood, New Jersey*

"The strategies shared within this book will transform a teacher's classroom or any educational organization. Moreover, these strategies are not something that is a new reform or something additional for teachers to implement. The ideas outlined are positive social and emotional responsive teaching techniques; under the leadership of Dr. Lori Desautels, Washington Township Schools has achieved both increased test scores and decreased negative behaviors in our classrooms.

"I have personally witnessed these strategies in action with students in our schools. As the person responsible for hiring in our great school district, I have seen that any candidate teacher or administrator who can speak to the neuroscience of teaching children certainly has a competitive edge over candidates who cannot.

"This book will transform the way you think and treat students as well as all individuals in your life."

*Mr. Thomas Oestreich, Director of Human Resources Metropolitan School District of Washington Township*

"Through compelling narrative, the authors shed light on the idea of debunking traditional approaches of school systems by illuminating building relationships with students that are humanistic, authentic, positive, and raw in nature. This must-read, inspirational book is filled with practical perspectives that are written *for* and *from* an educator perspective.

"A motivating reminder of how it is a great gift to be called a teacher, *Unwritten* encourages the reader to introduce 'sparks' into the lives of young students. This is the real truth of the power of the student /teacher relationship. Lori and Mike will give you real life examples of human connections and how this is the true key to learning.

"*Unwritten* is the best advice I could give to all my teachers to inspire all learners in their classrooms. I highly recommend to all my future teachers that they read about the untold value of human connections that is vital to all learning relationships."

*Pamela A. Vaughan, Ed.D., Asst. Dean, School of Education, Stockton University-Galloway Township, New Jersey*

"This book is a must-read for any preservice or inservice teachers, administrators, counselors, and other educators. The authors provide proven brain-based strategies for teaching and learning based on both their personal and other scientifically-based research that will help you support success for all students. *Unwritten* will enhance your knowledge and understanding in the growing field of mind-brain education."

*Diana Cheshire, Ph.D., Associate Dean, School of Education, Samford University*

"Like other soulful and timely descriptions of American schools, this work reminds us of why good educators enter and remain in the field, and what is needed to get back to that sacred purpose.

"This book could well become required reading in educator preparation programs and the basis for extended professional development work for classroom veterans and administrators across the nation. It is reflective, affirming, and grounded in research about how people learn and teach. And while the authors may rankle some educators, they will surely do what good educators always attempt to do — invite deeper thinking and understanding about what is most important in our lives."

*Frank Livoy, Associate Director, Delaware Center for Teacher Education*

"Desautels and McKnight offer a comprehensive review of what is wrong with the industrial paradigm as applied to education as well as a review of what new findings in brain science may have to offer educators as they develop alternatives to the current system. If you care about children and their education, read this book. It is helpful, hopeful and practical."

*Pat Dannenberg, Teacher, School Psychologist, Principal*

"*Unwritten* is an absolute critical read for the educators of today's children. *Unwritten* weaves together the 'stories' of our educational system, our educators, and our students; recognizing that we must honor each and all. The beauty of this book is that it focuses on the intricacies of teaching and learning including the power of emotions and the impact of hope. If we are truly committed to transforming education we must focus on our human connections."

**Ami Anderson, Coordinator of the ROOTS Program for Indianapolis Public Schools**

"I recently re-entered the field of Education after a five-year hiatus. It was challenging as I sensed 'the system' was in a state of flux and change, struggling to evolve and adapt. I felt overwhelmed and anxious. Reading *Unwritten* has inspired me and provided not only hope but also confirmed my faith that every student entering my classroom can and will thrive.

"*Unwritten* provides numerous tools to enhance teachers' positive social interactions with the children and teens that enter our classrooms daily; students who are secretly longing for someone to show them authentic belief and compassion. In short, this book is a guide to becoming a 'turn around teacher.'

"*Unwritten* provides fresh insights, support and encouragement during these times of change. Desautels' and McKnight's knowledge and foresight serve as a beacon, a 'Guiding Light' for the future of education. I truly appreciate the optimistic vision this book offers to teachers at all stages of their careers."

**Danielle Kessler, English Teacher, Atlantic County Institute of Technology**

# Unwritten

## THE STORY
## OF A
## LIVING SYSTEM

# Unwritten

## THE STORY OF A
## LIVING SYSTEM

*A Pathway to
Enlivening and Transforming
Education*

Lori L. Desautels, Ph.D.
Michael McKnight, M.A.

*Wyatt-MacKenzie Publishing*
DEADWOOD, OREGON

Unwritten, The Story of a Living System:
A Pathway to Enlivening and Transforming Education

Lori L. Desautels, Ph.D., Michael McKnight, M.A.

ISBN: 978-1-942545-10-1
Library of Congress Control Number: 2015946497

Edited by Denise C. Buschmann. Proofread by Karen Kibler.
Indexed by Matthew White.

*Wyatt-MacKenzie Publishing*
DEADWOOD, OREGON
www.WyattMacKenzie.com

**Publisher's Cataloging-in-Publication Data**

Desautels, Lori L.
    Unwritten, the story of a living system: a pathway to enlivening and transforming education/
Lori L. Desautels, Ph.D. and Michael McKnight, M.A.
    pages cm
    ISBN 978-1-942545-10-1
    Includes bibliographical references and index.

1. Educational change —United States. 2. Public schools —United States. 3. School improvement
programs —United States. 4. School management and organization. 5. School environment.
6. Curriculum change. I. McKnight, Michael, 1955-. II. Title.

LB2806.45.D47 2015
371.2 –dc23                                                                          2015946497

# PREFACE

*Unwritten* is about possibilities. Lori and Michael offer seven compelling stories to inspire educators to reflect upon their practices, their  beliefs about authentic learning, and their understanding of children's needs using connections as they learn. The stories expand and develop the basic premises of the book: Schools are living systems, alive with possibilities. When school and education are envisioned as teaching the whole child, and purpose drives the experiences, all children are able to not only achieve academic standards, but also can reach their full potential.

My experiences in schools with students, parents, teachers and administrators validate the authors' underlying themes. These themes embrace the concept that learning at all levels is relational and the core of success is grounded in personal connections. Lori and Michael provide the reader with inspirational quotes, topical dialogues, activities, and strategies, helping to connect the stories to their personal experiences and thoughts. The book does not provide the reader with answers to the questions that are common when discussing education today, but offers opportunities to connect with the realities facing educators today with fresh eyes.

*Unwritten, The Story of a Living System* is both practical and inspirational. It may be the book to read after a professional development opportunity introducing the latest curriculum to help a teacher put the new information in perspective. It may be the book a beginning teacher would read before stepping into the classroom for the first time. It may be the book a teacher educator would include to assist emerging teachers in the development of their personal philosophy of teaching. It may be the book an experienced and overwhelmed teacher would study to ignite the passion that has been compromised by years of teaching in an impersonal education system. Wherever we, as educators, may be on our career paths, Lori and Michael remind us of the importance and urgency of the work we are honored to do as teachers. Their words have the potential to guide our thinking and practices as we listen to children's calls, learn from children, and create brain-compatible learning environments for children. As educators we know, yet sometimes need to be reminded, that in part, the quality of children's futures depends upon us, the teachers.

Cynthia Jackson Ed.D.
District Positive Discipline Coordinator
Indianapolis Public Schools

# FOREWORD

*"Schools are alive and we are working, not as standardized machines, but within webs of human relationships."*

It seems that so much of the current education conversation is consumed by topics on school reform, teacher shortage, state and federal mandates and assessments. School improvement is often the overarching goal of these "reforms."

So you can only imagine the joy found in reading the book, *Unwritten: The Story of a Living System*, which is framed in hope, resilience and optimism for students, teaching and learning. This new book, written by consummate educators, Lori Desautels, Ph.D. and Michael McKnight, M.A., inspires and reminds me exactly why I chose a career in education.

Each chapter is full of brain-aligned practices, strategies, words, questions and ideas that build trust, engage students and connect the lives of teachers with their students. Thus, building on the strengths of students, rather than "finding and correcting deficits" in the system is celebrated throughout the book.

The journey of real educators sharing their daily challenges and successes allows us to see their "re-visioning" of education reform. This reminds us to give attention to the social and emotional bonds needed before meaningful learning can ever occur.

So how did this application of so much research, knowledge and desire become a reality? Let us step back in time for a bit....

A little over two years ago, Dr. Desautels (or as referred to by the students, "Dr. Lori") was introduced to me by a mutual friend, Tom Oestreich, a colleague in the Washington Township School district in Indianapolis, and one of her great fans. He shared that he had first met her as a parent where he served as a high school principal and knew I would value her renowned work in the application of brain research in the school setting. Her knowledge and strategies had already "wowed" the staff at his high school.

Enthralled from the moment I met her, it was evident that her background and knowledge, as both a former special education teacher and a professor of education at Marian University, made her a valuable resource for the schools where I served as Director of Elementary Education. We felt strongly that her current work would greatly enhance the already excellent teaching and learning occurring in the district. I assumed a traditional staff development model would be designed with her leading a team of teachers in the sharing of best brain practices in some sort of after-school experience.

I was stunned when she shared that she would like to co-teach, twice weekly, with one or two less experienced teachers at one of our local elementary schools for the semester. She believed the only way to ensure that her work would really have the desired effect on students was for her to use the co-teaching model with a teacher willing to try new strategies through co-teaching and observe the social and academic effect on the students. She believed this particular model of teaching would broaden her knowledge and credibility.

Suffice it to say, she began this teaching journey at one school and quickly was viewed as a major influence throughout the entire district. Her authenticity and real-life connections grew as she built strong relationships and taught classes of students, teachers, and regularly met with the principals. We could not get enough of her amazing ideas and strategies!

Marsha Reynolds
Education Consultant

*Authors' Note*:

While we wrote this book together, there are portions we wrote individually. We've added a note at the beginning of sections, so the reader will know whether it is both of us, "MICHAEL & LORI," or one writer specifically.

# The Story of a Living System

*I am because you are.*

UMBUTU

## MICHAEL & LORI

WE CANNOT REMEMBER a more chaotic and tenuous time in our nation's educational story. We are closing and opening schools, increasing the amount and intensity of standardized tests, changing education standards, starting more charter schools, magnet schools, and school choice programs. We are creating additional and elaborate teacher and administrator evaluation systems tied to achievement testing as well as "best practice" rubrics. We are changing school schedules, increasing the amount of time we teach certain subjects, and experimenting with year-round schooling. We are increasing the use of technology through-out the system, and despite all these efforts, there remains a sense that something is not quite right with our educational system. Quite possibly, for reasons we are not addressing, our schools are not working.

If we step back and widen our view, there are many countries throughout our planet that are attempting to "reform" their educational system. It has become a global concern.

Beneath all the tinkering that is being conducted around the globe, and particularly in our country, a worldview exists that sees our educational system as a predictable and manageable machine.

This machine can be controlled by providing certain "inputs" in the form of curriculum, topics, and core subjects, and by measuring "outputs" with additional assessments and testing. It is a worldview that is deeply embedded in how we perceive the world we inhabit. This perception of the world as a machine has influenced our thinking and the ways we initiate "how" to solve these problems. This perception shapes our institutions and our behaviors even if we are not aware of it. In our schools this worldview is based on finding and fixing deficits in our young people. Rarely do schools look and see "whole children." We have continued to focus all our "reform initiatives" on the peripheral fixes that have not and will not transform the current system. Why is this the case?

Could this worldview of fixing and remediating that we have focused upon be based on an illusion? It does not feel real or accurate. It has many of us looking at our schools as factories and our young people as "pieces" moving along assembly lines. It only sees "external" structures and does not see beneath human behavior.

Learning is the most natural thing human beings do. Yet, it seems the "harder" we work in schools helping our students acquire the learning they need, the more we see academic performances stay stagnant or lessen.

Schools are not machines. Schools are a network of human beings who feel, think, behave, and function within a human system that is alive and never static. Schools are living systems! This living system of sentient beings are neurobiologically wired to feel first, then to think, to love, to connect, and to experience deep joy as well as deep disappointment and pain. This system is wired to thrive, even through difficult times. *Have we lost our way through the primordial landscape of our innate purpose and genius?* We can begin to think and to feel differently. Deep learning is profoundly relational, and connection to one another is a prerequisite for our collective emotional, social, spiritual, and cognitive growth and development.

Our current story is rooted in scarcity and deficiency. This mindset leads to a prescriptive standardized process and structure of schooling that strikingly looks and feels the same all over America. Many of our children are not learning in this environment. Many children are dropping out of this system, and in many places, half of our students leave before graduating. One has to wonder why so many of our young people leave an institution that is supposed to benefit their lives? Students either formally leave by dropping out, or cognitively check out as they sit before us in our classrooms. At the same time, we are also witnessing an ever-increasing tendency toward violence. Our children are literally killing each other at younger and younger ages.

Programs do not change people. People change people. It is critical to remember that the schools we are working within consist of webs of relationships. The schools we work in are alive! Transformation within any living system cannot be externally mandated or directed. It can only be provoked. If we are to intimately connect to the hearts and minds of one another, change must come from within. We can create generative learning environments that invite learning that increases our capacity for continuous growth and development throughout our entire life-span. This will require a new way of looking at the world.

Deep learning, true learning, in human beings is profoundly relational. Close connections and attachment to supportive adults is a prerequisite to learning from them. Michael and I hope to disturb your thinking gently—gently enough to have you consider that your role as an educator is moving in a new direction inside a story that embraces the teaching and learning process that is organically alive, that inhales and exhales, that moves and grows within an adaptive messy context of a living system.

Please join us in dialogue as we question, remember, strategize, and rewrite *the story*. The story of a living system that knows compassion, that feels the joys and suffering of humankind, but oftentimes, loses its way in an industrial robotic environment where people are unable to thrive.

We have created a format for reading and digesting the content inside this book. We hope to bring these ideas to life by presenting specific teaching principles and strategies designed, not only to engage the students' intellect, but to trigger an emotional and relational link to their teachers and classmates, as well.

Within each chapter, we have included a quote, the content topics interspersed with a dialogue between the two of us. As we wrote this story, we discussed, questioned, and shared our thoughts. It is our hope that in the ways this story was created, you too will benefit from this book's dialogue and actionable "sparks" at the end of each chapter. The teaching sparks are strategies that are aligned to the topics in each section. We entitled these as "sparks" to ignite your enthusiasm, while providing you with resources to assist you in your current educational practices. Michael and I understand what the research reports. *We learn deeply when we teach others.* As we write, we also learn. We are not the experts; we consider ourselves, learners and teachers. We share your passion and questions about how to enliven and improve this current, beautifully complex, living system.

# TABLE OF CONTENTS

## The System Story

We have been discussing, arguing, debating and changing the educational system repeatedly for many years. We have increased assessment, tied student growth to test scores, and created standards, technology and a curriculum with a heavy emphasis on English Language Arts, Math, and Science. We have created zero tolerance policies in our schools since the Columbine tragedy and we have placed national transition to teaching programs into many of our schools and districts. We are still struggling. The mechanistic and system story has forgotten that education is a living system and emotional connection brings learning, teaching and policy to life!

## The Story of the Educator

We cannot fix another person, and in trying to, we disrespect the journey of another. Teaching is a vocation rooted in communication and emotions. When we try and quantify relationships, student and teacher growth, movement and feelings, we have lost sight of masterful teaching. Research repeatedly reports that the difference between a good teacher and a superior teacher is one who self-reflects. The Story of the Educator is one who understands how powerful, healing, and contagious emotions are when sitting beside children and adolescents.

## The Student's Story

Our students bring their stories into our classrooms. They carry in so much more than we can ever know. The master teacher understands the private logic, beliefs, culture and fears our children and adolescents bring into an environment where math and language are often times taught in isolation. We cannot teach them, if we cannot reach them! In this chapter, we delve into the personal lives of our students embracing their stories as we create instruction that personalizes and brings the emotional and cognitive worlds to life!

## The Story of Emotions

The title of this chapter is stated in the sequence of importance as we address the teaching and learning process. Brain research has now discovered that not only are emotions contagious but mirror neurons are activated in the brain when we observe and ingest the behaviors and dispositions of others. This is the organic component of the teaching and learning dynamic. Our ability to problem solve, predict, emotionally regulate and organize our thought processes are completely shut off and down if the stress response system is chronically or even minimally activated for long periods of time. Many of our children and adolescents are walking into our classrooms in a chronic stress response brain state. The fear, worries, frustration and anxiety so many of us feel for lengthy periods of time prohibit our ability for sustainable learning. This chapter takes a detailed look at the power of emotional connection and brain states for learning.

## The Story of Active Hope

Brain plasticity is our brain's ability to create new neural pathways and connections based upon experiences. The experiences and environments we create in our schools and classrooms play a significant role in the emotional social and cognitive well-being of all students and teachers. To feel "felt" is the greatest gift we can give to one another. Stephanie Pace Marshall describes it best in this chapter.

*To educate our children wisely requires that we create generative life affirming learning communities, by design. These communities are grounded in the principles of life and learning and have their roots in: purpose, not prescription; meaning not memory; engagement, not transmission; inquiry, not compliance; questions, not answers; exploration, not acquisition; personalization, not uniformity; interdependence, not individualism; collaboration, not competition; challenge, not threat; and trust and joy, not fear.*

STEPHANIE PACE MARSHALL

### The Story of Well-Being

We see students survive every day. We often times survive every day. We survive a class, a test, a conflict, a relationship and a challenge; and yet, surviving is not thriving! If the brain is in a survival response; its creative, resourceful and imaginative higher level thought processes are compromised because of emotions and thoughts that feel unsafe and threatening. When we feel guilt, shame, anger, sadness and any negative emotion over an extended period of time our brains begin to create neural pathways that ignite habits of feelings in response to the thoughts that call forth these emotions. Hope is defined as a feeling or expectation and desire for a certain thing to happen. When we model hope for our students, we share the heartaches, celebrations, and every emotion that has occurred inside the steps we have taken for goals we desire to teach. Hope begins with questions. When we question our goals, plans and intentions, we help develop them.

What do you hope for today? What do you hope for this week? How do you get there? What will it take to make this desire a reality? Is the hope you have for this relationship, experience, or event something you can work towards? Is your "hope" something you can control? If the hope lies outside our control, then we must model for our students what is within our power and control. We must help one another to understand that hope is the roadmap in a destination of perspective.

**The Story of Now**

In this final chapter, Michael and I discuss and design a story for education that emphasizes creativity, perceptual data, and instruction that aligns with the neural circuitry of each child and adolescent's unique brain. We discuss ways to build emotional connection assisting youth in overcoming adverse environments. The emphasis in this chapter includes principles, strategies, and tangible models that engage, motivate and inspire learners and educators. The story of now reaches out to teacher and parent well-being as well as student development.

*The future for education is not in standardizing*
*but in customizing; not in promoting groupthink and*
*"de-individuation" but in cultivating the real depth*
*and dynamism of human abilities of every sort.*

KEN ROBINSON, *THE ELEMENT: HOW FINDING YOUR*
*PASSION CHANGES EVERYTHING*

# CHAPTER ONE

# The System Story

## MICHAEL

IMAGINE YOURSELF WALKING into any public or private school in our country. It does not matter what level the school might be—elementary, middle, or high school. Imagine just wandering around the school. Walk down the hallways, visit the cafeteria, go in the gym, visit the library, and move in and out of the classrooms. As you wander around, you may begin to notice that the majority of places we call schools are very similar. For the most part, they all look and feel the same. Students have teachers that teach various subjects. Students are grouped by their age, subjects are taught separately, class begins and ends during a specific period of time, bells ring, and students move on. Tests are taken, report cards and grades are given, students are sorted and ranked, and children that fall behind are placed in special programs to be remediated.

It really would be difficult to tell what state you are in simply by walking around a school. They are all arranged in a very similar manner. Principals are in charge of the buildings, and often the assistant principal continues to posit "discipline," as grade level teachers are sorted by their "content expertise." The state standards and curriculum guides all look very much the same. The lesson plans teachers write all look similar. Apart from some novel technologies such as computers, smart boards, flat screen televisions, handheld devices, and a host of ever changing new devices and platforms for teachers and students, schools are not that much different than they were three decades ago. What occurs in most schools and classrooms has not changed that much, even with new technologies. How can this be?

Underneath the "sameness" we perceive in many of our schools, there is a collective worldview concerning how human beings learn. The present-day view of learning originated during the Industrial Revolution when learning was first viewed as mechanistic and machine-like. This worn out model was partially successful a hundred years ago, however, students' evolving emotional, social, and individual cognitive needs were not addressed. The Industrial Revolution refers to the new manufacturing processes and rapid developments that took place in technology and industry during the eighteenth and nineteenth centuries. The term also refers to the many deep-rooted changes in the way people lived and worked. Education followed this model. Mass production techniques, made possible by technological development, required setting up large factories with a large work force of adults and children. There was a much greater production and division of labor during this time, but there was little awareness and attention paid to the developmental needs of children and adolescents. In 1938, for the first time, the Fair Labor

Standards Act regulated the minimum age and maximum hours of child laborers and mandated compulsory school attendance to twelve years of age.

Picture an assembly line. The students move along through the system as if they are pieces on the assembly line. As they progress, the teacher inputs specific content, aligned with academic standards that the student is to learn and know in an explicit period of time. Curriculum and Instructional Directors spend time aligning curriculum to grade level expectations. Students are prodded along attempting to acquire the content expectations for their grade level. As students advance, they are tested and graded on those content expectations, traversing from one grade to the next with their peer group. Teachers deliver instruction and they manage classrooms as "efficiently" and "effectively" as possible. Any student falling behind is recognized and removed from the assembly line. With removal, they may be "fixed" or remediated, then placed back onto the line. Often students are treated as passive receptacles of information and knowledge delivered by the teacher. These bits and pieces of disconnected information become sterile and moot as our young move from one classroom to another. As students progress, they continue to be ranked and sorted against their age group peers. Graduation follows after a certain amount of time spent in school and once they have mastered the ability to answer a number of correct questions on one of the many assessment stops along the way.

> *In all affairs it's a healthy thing now and then*
> *to hang a question mark on the things*
> *you have long taken for granted.*
> BERTRAND RUSSELL

Many of us feel something is not right with the majority of our schools. Having been in the education profession for over thirty years, I have witnessed many innovations designed to transform our schools. We tinker with existing structures, changing schedules, extending the length of the school day, designing new curriculum guides, providing more professional development for our teachers as testing continues to increase. We open magnet schools, charter schools, and various academies with specialized learning programs and curriculums. We call for smaller class sizes, vouchers, on-line schools, "highly qualified teachers," while initiating year-round school calendars. We have introduced and implemented progress monitoring assessments, along with the addition of remedial classes, attempting to revamp our current system. Technology continues to evolve inside our schools for assessment, remediation, and instruction. Our students are spending more and more time being directly instructed and assessed by machines. Special Education is a field that continues to change and evolve.

"After decades of steady increases, the population of students with disabilities peaked in 2004-05 with 6.72 million youngsters, comprising [sic] 13.8 percent of the nation's student population. The following year marked the first time since the enactment of the Individuals with Disabilities Education Act (IDEA) that special-education participation numbers declined—and they have continued to do so, falling to 6.48 million students by 2009-10, or 13.1 percent of all students nationwide."[1] It is not rare, however, to have school districts where the classification rates soar above 20 percent. That translates into one out of every five students in need of a special education. One might ask what kind of system creates a need for that many students to be classified as eligible for a specialized education? Research also makes us very aware of the links between race, poverty, and special education rates.

We create teacher and principal evaluation systems that link professional evaluations into "best practices," correlating these metrics with monitoring student growth through assessments and determining teacher effectiveness. We have created basic skills programs, remedial programs, special education programs, after school programs, alternative school programs. We have transitioned from chalk boards to white boards, from overhead projectors to smart boards, from desk tops to lap tops to bring-your-own devices; yet, none of the changes we have made have come close to transforming our schools. Fundamentally, the story has stayed the same.

This mechanistic worldview drives the way we educate our young and sees schooling as simply the "transmission of knowledge" from one person—the teacher, to another—the student. This way of "seeing" education and schooling continues to be the dominant and mainstream approach to schooling in our country. Ron Miller defines the transmission model of schooling this way:

*"Knowledge is seen as an established, objective, authoritative body of facts outside the learner's experiences or personal preferences, and the role of the educator is to transmit this knowledge, along with accompanying academic skills and attitudes, to the learner's mind."*[2]

Historically, the current story of the expansion of public education and the design of almost all our schools was based on the need to create modern factory workers. This was the time when standardization became synonymous with "modern." It was the time of Henry Ford's assembly line and, at the time, a more modern form of work. It was in this context that the current story of education was born, the birthplace of "modern schooling."

We unconsciously institutionalize this worldview in our thinking and our behavior. In essence the world viewed as a machine continues to shape our institutions and the majority of our schools at every developmental level. It is not that difficult to step back and imagine a child placed on the "assembly line" in kindergarten, shuffling along through the system with a final destination of being "college and career ready."

The current wave of school reform movements across our country and the globe are simply creating a twenty-first century assembly line system. We seem to believe we are moving forward but our gaze continues to be driven by deeply held and often unconscious views of schooling, teaching, and learning. These unconscious perceptions are looking backward, not forward. If we observe closely, there is really nothing new in the current school reform story. It continues to "see" all students as the same. The current story is rooted in deficiency, scarcity, and remediation. We have focused and almost perfected our ability to find what is wrong with our young people. What is the outcome of the current story of education? This system has not and will not serve us well. The majority of students leaving this mechanistic schooling feel less than adequate intellectually. Most celebrate being finished with their schooling so that they can get on with their "real life." Many also feel they are finally done with learning! Only a small fraction of students leave feeling that their gifts were recognized after spending thirteen years in a place called school.

Our current story continues to shut down learning, which is the most natural thing human beings do. The myth that at one time our public schools were a place of great engagement and learning, is just that—a myth. Our current high school graduation rate is approximately 75 percent, and that is as high as it has ever been. An estimated one million students will fail to graduate this year, which is a loss of 5,500 students for every day on the academic calendar.[3]

When we actually take the time to ask students about their schooling, the answers we receive should give any adult interested in education major concern. According to a national report, Charting A Path from Engagement to Achievement, a 2009 survey of 42,000 high school students reported that 66 percent of students stated they are bored every day in school. The students consistently cite that the material is boring and not relevant. The students also indicated, with a whopping 82 percent in agreement, that they would welcome more opportunities to be creative at school.[4]

This old story of schooling stifles real learning, and cuts off our young's natural learning capacities to explore, to create, and to imagine. It literally shuts down the most natural thing human beings do.

It is time for a new story of education and schooling in our country. So let us imagine another trip through another imaginary school. As you wander around this school, try and go underneath all the surface activities of the school. Notice the content that is being taught, the bells that ring, the tests being taken, the pencils being sharpened, the lectures being delivered, and the questions being asked. Notice the lockers being opened, the lesson plans being delivered and just stop and listen. Observe and feel the place you are in. Listen to the buzz and hustling of all the life within this place we call a school. Feel the pulse of the place you have entered. Sense the vibrations and energy within the walls. *All schools have a felt sense.*

Schools are living systems, and they are alive. Viewing our schools as living systems creates space for seeing our role within them much differently. We do not need to restructure schools or reconstitute them. We do not need to remediate or fix them.

### MICHAEL & LORI

*What we need is a Re-visioning of our schools.*

### A New Story

Knowing what we now know from a variety of academic, health, science, business and industry studies, along with the current educational research, we can no longer continue to do what we are doing to "reform" our educational system. The current emphasis on reform needs to move toward transformation; otherwise, we are just tinkering around the edges of a system that is stuck in a misguided collective view of learning. Transformation requires that we "see" and "think" differently. Our schools are living systems, not machines. The older reform story treats those within the walls of our educational institutions as things rather than as living, breathing human beings. It views teaching and learning as linear and predictable. As long as this remains the priority focus of our work, we will remain stuck inside a mechanistic view of school reform that simply will never work. As educator Dr. Stephanie Pace Marshall has reminded us: "Based on an outdated and erroneous understanding of how we learn, create, and innovate within human systems, decades of reform and school restructuring have not transformed our system of schooling or the nature and quality of our children's learning and thinking. And by design, it cannot. Knowing what we now know we can no longer do what we now do." She goes on to state that, "We must nurture decidedly different minds."[5]

Deep learning is profoundly relational. Students, teachers, parents, and administrators form networks that are embedded in systems that are alive. For our young people to learn deeply, it is a prerequisite for them to be attached to caring adults who are able to "see" and meet their deepest learning needs. Programs, curriculums, materials, and technologies do not change people; only people change people. Our brains are literally wired to connect with one another. Social connections have always been critical for human beings; without these connections, we would never have survived our evolutionary journey.

Dr. Mathew Lieberman, a professor and director of the Social Cognitive Neuroscience Lab at UCLA, has been researching this topic for over a decade. Based on his lab's research in social neuroscience, Lieberman concludes that our need to connect with other people is even more fundamental than our basic need for food and shelter. He has been bold enough to state that Abraham Maslow was wrong, that social connection is the building block from which all our other human needs are met. This includes our very human need to learn and grow. Lieberman's research concludes that human beings are motivated by our drive for social connection. He states that given what we know about the social brain creating the right social environments, in our workplaces (and our schools), this should be the top priority for anyone who wants to bring out the best in themselves and others. Getting more "social" is the key to increased learning.[6]

What our children and adolescents deserve, is an educational system that is filled with caring, competent, and wise adults who recognize and value their students' unique needs and abilities. Our young need to be nurtured in school environments where they feel cared for, competent, and valued for who they are. A stellar educational system recognizes their strengths and their gifts and helps them to cultivate those special abilities. The resiliency research supports the idea that discussions about educational reform and transformation cannot be limited to discussions about best practices as reflected in new curricula and new programs. Resiliency is the ability to persist in the face of adversity or the ability to bounce back after facing a challenging situation. Helping students develop resiliency skills and attitudes has a positive effect on academic achievement, behavior, and long-term success in life. How can this be supported in schools? A positive connection with supportive adults or "turnaround teachers" is directly linked to student resiliency. The central finding of resiliency research is that young people living within "risky systems" can overcome the odds if they are nurtured within another micro system that provides a safe environment, and at the very minimum, one adult who is tenaciously and consistently caring.[7]

Today more than ever, we have many students sitting before us in classrooms all across our country who are in desperate need of adult support, nurturing, and connection in their lives. They will not learn from us until we make these connections. These young people are living in and attempting to navigate environments of very high stress. The research in neuroscience reminds us that when the brain is chronically activated in the stress response system, our ability to think is literally turned off.

*There can be no keener revelation of a society's soul
than the way it treats its children.*

NELSON MANDELA

Questions drive all learning. As we begin to look at our current educational system we begin with this direct and simple question: Does America have disposable children and young people? Every day in America more than 185 children are arrested for violent crimes, over 4,000 children are arrested, seven children are killed by guns, four children are killed by abuse or neglect, over 1,800 are confirmed as abused or neglected, over 16,000 students are suspended from school, and approximately 8,000 students drop out of our schools.[8]

After only a cursory look at the current state of our children and youth, the answer to the opening question is a resounding and very sad, yes. Yes, America currently has many disposable children. These are America's disposable young. They have been caught in a perpetual cycle of violence and pain. They live with chronic toxic levels of stress in their lives—stress levels high enough to change the dynamics of the brain. They are unattached, adult-leery, and very reluctant to trust anyone.

There is one major institution that continues to touch almost all of our children and adolescents. This institution is the public school system. Ninety percent of our young people continue to be enrolled in our public school system. It is the only institution that will have an opportunity to help shape the lives of our future citizens. All of the students who enter our schools are really citizens in embryo, yet, our current system itself does not recognize or know what to do with these young people.

These are the children who continue to cause us the

most difficulty in our schools and our classrooms. These children and young people are in pain, and what we see as problem behavior is actually "pain-based behaviors." Pain-based behaviors are driven by deep pain. These oppositional, defiant, and oftentimes unmotivated, and apathetic behaviors are exhibited by young people who have been deeply hurt. Hurt people hurt people. Hurt people do not learn very well in our schools.

Many of us working in our school systems across the country are unintentionally participating in and perpetuating cycles of violence with our most deeply hurt and neglected young people. They enter our classrooms and schools on a daily basis, causing us to quickly become engaged in escalating conflicts. These are the students who we call unmotivated, disturbed, at risk, disobedient, and disrespectful. We continue to blame what we label as their dysfunctional families and throw up our arms in defeat.

Schools have never had much success with these young people—our most troubled and vulnerable children. The history of schools and the children in pain has been historically negative. The latest discipline trends continue to focus on zero tolerance policies, separation to other programs, and so-called boot camps that misunderstand and mistreat our already mistreated young people.

Many of these young people end up in our prison system. "One in every three black males born today can expect to go to prison at some point in their life, compared with one in every six Latino males, and one in every 17 white males, if current incarceration trends continue." These are among the many pieces of evidence cited by the Sentencing Project, a Washington, D.C.- based group that advocates for prison reform.[9]

We have many states that now have policies in place that have students repeating grade levels for their inability to pass standardized tests. We have young adolescents who have gone through their entire school system, passed their courses, and still cannot get a high school diploma because of their inability to pass these "high stakes tests."

An article in *Education Week*, "Holding Kids Back Doesn't Help Them" by Deborah Stipek and Michael Lombardo (2014), states that:

"State-mandated retention statutes are being enacted at a dizzying pace by legislatures across the country. In 2012, 13 states adopted laws targeting early reading achievement, many of which require schools to hold back elementary school students based on reading assessments. At least 10 other states have considered or are considering similar laws."

There remains compelling evidence that retention practices increase the likelihood of students later dropping out of school. Stipek and Lombardo go on to say " . . . an examination of the best research conducted on the effects of retention demonstrates that the policy is most likely counterproductive." They cite a 2005 review of decades of studies by Nailing Xia and Elizabeth Glennie: "Research has consistently found that retained students are at a higher risk of leaving school earlier, even after controlling for academic performance and other factors such as race and ethnicity, gender, socioeconomic status, family background, etc."[10]

If one were to step back and contemplate the overall strategies employed and executed when working with these young people, it might be summarized as one of a "scare and punish them into straightening out." This philosophy has never worked well with humans, yet it continues to drive policy as well as behavior. If these scare and punish tactics do not work, and we cannot find compliance, we simply continue to expel them to nowhere.

> *The hurt that troubled children create is never*
> *greater than the hurt they feel.*
> L. TOBIN

Underneath the behaviors of these children, who come to hate and eventually sometimes to hurt others, are children who experienced threats, rejection, and mistreatment from the adults in their lives rather than encouragement and love. These children have been deprived of the oxygen of healthy human development—love. Could one even imagine a more pessimistic view of working with society's most vulnerable children?

As Larry Brendtro states:

*"Communities of civility do not mass produce disrespectful children. Positive social control comes from social bonds between people who care for one another."*[11]

In stark contrast to our current culture, many indigenous cultures historically revered their young. Other cultures, many of which we term primitive, have a very different view of their children. Terminology in the Maori culture of New Zealand that describes a child is literally translated as a "gift of the gods." No one would throw away or dispose of a "gift from the gods." Traditionally in the Maori culture, children were seen as the children of the whole tribe or group, not just belonging to their mother and father. Children were raised in, and supported by a wider group that included grandparents, aunts and uncles, as well as parents.

Raising healthy Maori children requires not just

parents who are able and willing to nurture their children, but also a wider social and economic support system. This is especially true if parents experience poverty, social exclusion, or marginalization.[12]

The Lakota people are an indigenous tribe of the Great Plains of North America. In the Lakota language, the word for a child is "wakanjeja." It literally translates as "sacred being." We may want to reflect on how we describe our students in our schools and classrooms every day. Do we treat everyone in our educational institutions as sacred beings? For the Lakota culture, the responsibility of raising a child was given to the entire community, and not just limited to a child's mother and father. In fact, uncles and aunts also had parental duties in caring for their nieces and nephews. In many of these unified and holistic cultures, the raising of their young was a community endeavor.

*In Native American cultures, spiritual concepts*
*are completely intertwined with the secular.*
*In fact, we make no distinction between body and soul,*
*which is a Greek concept.*

MARTIN BROKENLEG
Native American author and educator

One needs to ask oneself, what if we treated all youth we come in contact with as "sacred beings"? What would that require from us? What would that look, sound, and feel like? We need to find ways to turn away from the current deficit-driven model of schooling, where our focus is to find what is wrong with our young people and "fix" them. We need to turn our teaching toward "connection" where many of our finest educators have found relationships with their students that are paving the paths for significant learning that begins with the students' strengths.

*Creating a respectful, caring, and intentionally inviting learning environment is the surest way to encourage student achievement.*

JANE BLUESTEIN

## MICHAEL

I am reminded of a story I read written by George H. Reavis. Reavis was an Assistant Superintendent of the Cincinnati Public Schools in the 1940s. I believe this story is as relevant today as it was when it was first written—maybe more so.

### The Animal School: A Fable by George Reavis

*Once upon a time the animals decided they must do something heroic to meet the problems of a "new world," so they organized a school. They had adopted an activity curriculum consisting of running, climbing, swimming, and flying. To make it easier to administer the curriculum, all the animals took all the subjects.*

*The duck was excellent in swimming, in fact, better than his instructor. But he made only passing grades in flying and was very poor in running. Since he was slow in running, he had to stay after school and also drop swimming in order to practice running. This was kept up until his webbed feet were badly worn, and he was only average in swimming. But average was acceptable in school so nobody worried about that, except the duck.*

*The rabbit started at the top of the class in running but had a nervous breakdown because of so much makeup work in swimming.*

*The squirrel was excellent in climbing until he developed frustration in the flying class where his teacher made him start from the ground up instead of the treetop down. He also developed a "charlie horse" from overexertion and then got a C in climbing and a D in running.*

*The eagle was a problem child and was disciplined severely. In the climbing class, he beat all the others to the top of the tree but insisted on using his own way to get there.*

*At the end of the year, an abnormal eel that could swim exceedingly well and also run, climb, and fly a little, had the highest average and was valedictorian.*

*The prairie dogs stayed out of school and fought the tax levy because the administration would not add digging and burrowing to the curriculum. They apprenticed their children to a badger and later joined the groundhogs and gophers to start a successful private school.*

Does this fable have a moral?[13]

Sacred beings do not need to be repaired. They need to be loved and loved well. They need to have their strengths and their gifts recognized and validated as they work on their less strong gifts. Love is a word that is rarely used when describing great teachers, but it is what great teachers do. Great teachers love their students, love the material they teach, and love working with and supporting the growth of young people

> *When you help, you see life as weak. When you fix,*
> *you see life as broken. When you serve, you see life as whole.*
> *Fixing and helping may be the work of the ego,*
> *and service the work of the soul.*
> RACHEL NAOMI REMEN

The kind of love great teachers have is related to serving their students well and seeing them as whole human beings. Caring, connected relationships are the key that allows one to begin the journey of becoming a "turnaround teacher" in the lives of our children and youth. This connection is critical and becomes crucial with our most troubled students. Why? First, loving support meets the core needs of all human beings—the need for emotional and physical safety. This is the foundational need of all humans. Our most troubled children have not had this need met in "sufficient ways." Great turnaround teachers have a fundamentally positive regard for all their students, even the students who enter classrooms extremely reluctant to enter relationships with adults. Simply put, your most troubled students do not learn from adults who do not care about them! Turnaround teachers forge connections with relationship-resistant young people.

*It is obvious that children will work harder and do things—even odd things like adding fractions—for people they love and trust.*

NEL NODDING

We can begin to think of the actions of Love in the classroom using this acronym:

**L**—stands for liberating. The kind of liberation love provides that another human being can come to rest within, the liberation to know that it is OK to be who you are in this classroom. As Gordon Neufeld says, "We liberate children not by making them work for our love but by letting them rest in it."

**O**—stands for oneness. Oneness is connection. We are all connected. We are social beings with social brains and we are literally wired to connect, to learn, to live, and to feel.

**V**—stands for validation. Validation is like oxygen for

the spirit and the soul. To be validated is to been "seen." Validation provides a felt sense that another human being has seen who you are, has understood you, affirmed and appreciated you for simply being you.

E—stands for evolving. To become more and more who you are and to continue to unfold into ever changing complex forms of yourself is to grow and develop. Our most difficult and troubled students have not experienced enough of this kind of love.

**Author and educator Tracy Kidder shares these words:** "Teachers usually have no way of knowing that they have made a difference in a child's life, even when they have made a dramatic one. But for children who are used to thinking of themselves as stupid or not worth talking to or deserving rape and beatings, a good teacher can provide an astonishing revelation. A good teacher can give a child at least a chance to feel, 'She thinks I'm worth something. Maybe I am.' Good teachers put snags in the river of children passing by, and over the years, they redirect hundreds of lives. Many people find it easy to imagine unseen webs of malevolent conspiracy in the world, and they are not always wrong. But there is also an innocence that conspires to hold humanity together, and it is made up of people who can never fully know the good that they have done."[14]

## A PRESENTATION BY LORI

### A Living System: Opening Words to my Students Spring Semester (2014)

You cannot fix a child or a system, nor should you, as you unintentionally disrespect one's journey. To foster resilience in children, we must first take a hard long look at "how" we can foster resilience inside our own lives. Yes, every child does deserve a fabulous education, but that education must begin with building trust, knowing our triggers, knowing that the behaviors and words expressed may be the tip of the iceberg. This is the tip that is daring and beckoning us to shatter the pain. Hurt people hurt people. Are we ready to search the turbulent waters inside our own lives that have brought us to a place where teaching in 2014 is the most honorable and privileged profession that has yet been recognized? You will enter your classrooms and your undergraduate and graduate coursework with choices, coupled with the neurobiology to change your own thinking. This perspective flexibility allows us to teach to the heart and mind of every individual that walks through our doors. "We teach who we are," but sometimes that is not enough, and it takes more courage to teach *who we are not.*

Over the past few months, I have learned deeply. My students were paramount teachers as I was privileged to share a part of their interior worlds, their "private logic" that is a culmination of all accumulated beliefs, experiences, values, thoughts, and feelings. This "inner world" is often kept tucked away unless an environment, a "space," is created in such a way that allows for feelings of safety and an untainted sense of belongingness. When any child or adult enters into a space that accepts, inspires, and affirms their "ever changing personhood," we have finally found the key that unlocks the door to extravagant learning. What is that key? That golden key is connection.

Creating a "space" for connections is valuable, sustainable, and a necessity inside this current system of education. Within our public schools across the world and country, there rests a paradox. We push, compete, strive, and teach to the academic tests that will supposedly improve our economies creating a global, competitive, and motivating market of individuals. Yes, there is another story. This story is told and felt by us. It is the story of well-being where we desire to create, design, play, breathe deeply, and "feel." When our positive emotions are felt and expressed, there is a contagious syndrome that knows how to spread and connect with others. We are neurobiologically wired to feel the laughter, heartbeats, and suffering of our fellow human beings. Our students desire to feel better than they do. We are a living system, a system that breathes, makes room, and shifts to improved feelings because people change people, not programs.

In many ways, our education system is often experienced by educators and students as mechanistic. We move in lines, we sit in spaces that tell us when to think, how to think, and we move in lines listening for the bells. We feel a disconnected and hollow "mindset" that exudes a ubiquitous air of doing, going, accomplishing, assessing, and repeating it all the very next day. We have forgotten our commonalities and the emotional engines that drive all we think and do. We all are so busy! My question is busy doing what? How are we spending our time and energy? What spaces have we created for rest, reflection, and renewal to build "resiliency" that is our natural birthright?

Connection is wired into our neural circuitry. We are social beings, and we have evolved and thrived through thousands of years based on this brain potential. Connection or lack thereof drives all relationships, emotion, and learning in life. How does connection occur? Can it be taught? How long does it take? What do I do when there are just some students who truly make it feel impossible to even begin to feel a sense of connection or a mutual joining? Yes, it can be taught and nurtured. It can be taught, modeled, and reflected upon with an intentionally created space that fosters our emotional health. This is a space that invites authentic discernment while building and fostering a repertoire of veritable perspectives.

Dr. Dan Seigel, author and psychiatrist, speaks of a mindset that is critically important to every human being as we look at engagement, motivation, and those social and emotional skills that drive all learning. "Feeling felt" is connection. When we "feel felt" by another, we no longer experience isolation or those lonely emotions of exclusion. "Feeling felt" by peers in the adolescent years overrides almost every behavior or conscious social choice. "Belonging matters most."

## LORI
### Exercise in Connection

Last semester in all my classes, I shared an ancient story of an African tribal tradition, which is located at the end of this chapter. Following the sharing of this ancient story with fifth graders, the students were beyond excited to share their "songs," the words that expressed their identities. As a part of their writing standards covering sentence conventions, they wrote their "identity" songs during the second semester of the school year.

When I recited this story to my undergraduates, I asked them to spend a few minutes pondering and writing their "song," the best parts of who they are. Collecting them at the end of class, I actually forgot about them until ten minutes before the evening graduate class began. I noticed the stack of wrinkled half sheets of paper from the afternoon stuffed inside a folder, and I began to read.

I could barely breathe, let alone speak, as their responses were so vulnerable. Poetry, two or three word descriptors, and slogans splattered the torn sheets of paper as their innermost thoughts spilled out.

Closing our graduate class, I randomly shared the songs and words of my undergraduate students. These responses left these second year teachers speechless. We discussed the power of story, the questions that diffuse rising anger, angst, and discomfort. After the students had read each of these responses, I reminded them, "Take this story, take your story, and begin connecting with your students, creating a space that uncovers their strengths, fears, hearts, and genius minds!" We closed class. We were all greatly touched, quietly pondering the expressed openness of these eighteen- to twenty-year-olds who taught us deeply on this Thursday evening.

Connection. It begins with the sharing of our human stories followed by the deep listening that lies beyond words, never requiring a verbal response. When we share our stories, taking the time to listen beyond the world of our lexicon, we begin to join hands, hearts, and thoughts around the table of extravagant learning. Below is the tribal story I shared and a few of the anonymous responses from the students.

How do we do this?

We do this through sharing our stories, followed by the deepest kind of listening that usually escapes most of us. When we share a personal narrative, a story that brings forth our commonalities as humans, we connect on the most intimate level. We begin to empathize—feeling what it must be like to walk in the clothing, shoes, and heart of another.

### The Himba, Namibia, & the Birth Song

There is a tribe in Africa where the birth date of a child is counted not from when they were born, nor from when they are conceived but from the day that the child was a thought in its mother's mind. And when a woman decides that she will have a child, she goes off and sits under a tree, by herself, and she listens until she can hear the song of the child who wants to come. And after she's heard the song of this child, she comes back to the man who will be the child's father, and teaches it to him. And then, when they make love to physically conceive the child, some of that time, they sing the song of the child as a way to invite it.

And then, when the mother is pregnant, the mother teaches that child's song to the midwives and the old women of the village, so that when the child is born, the old women and the people around her sing the child's song to welcome it. And then, as the child grows up, the other villagers are taught the child's song. If the child falls, or hurts its knee, someone picks it up and sings its song to it. Or perhaps the child does something wonderful, or goes through the rites of puberty, then as a way of honoring this person, the people of the village sing his or her song.

In the African tribe there is one other occasion upon which the villagers sing to the child. If at any time during his or her life, the person commits a crime or aberrant social act, the individual is called to the center of the village and the people in the community form a circle around them. Then they sing their song to them.

The tribe recognizes that the correction for antisocial behavior is not punishment; it is love and the remembrance of identity. When you recognize your own song, you have no desire or need to do anything that would hurt another.

And, it goes this way through their life. In marriage, the songs are sung together. And finally, when this child is lying in bed, ready to die, all the villagers know his or her song, and they sing—for the last time—the song to that person.

Responses from my undergraduate students:

"My phrase would be 'He would give you the shirt off his back.' It may not be a song, but it describes my life, because no matter friend or enemy, I will always help people in need."

"Five dollars? You got it! Food? You got it! I will never throw someone away. Show people you love, and love itself will return the favor."

"I am a survivor of an unimaginable childhood, but because of that, I am compassionate, understanding, and wholeheartedly free to help others—help them through their pain. I was born to serve."

## ∾ S P A R K S ∾

The teaching sparks for this chapter reside within the Himba story. Share this story with your students during any point in the school year. This story could also be shared with the families of the students. After listening and discussing the story as a class, the students can create their own "birth song." This exercise/assignment could be shared in poetry, music lyrics, a short story, or a shared mantra or motto. This spark is for all grade levels and ages. The class needs to be somewhat established and relationships should be solidified prior to this exercise in connection. Enjoy!

# CHAPTER 2

# The Story of the Educator

*Teaching, like any truly human activity, emerges from*
*one's inwardness, for better or worse. As I teach, I project the*
*condition of my soul onto my students, my subject,*
*and our way of being together.*

PARKER PALMER

## LORI

THE EDUCATOR'S STORY is one that I feel is universal. It is filled with our commonalities and perceived differences masked in moments of joy, frustrations, attachments to outcomes, as well as a perpetual longing for something more intimate or perhaps, more positive. This is human nature. From this perspective, I strive to be gentler with myself and gentler with all other beings who share the space in this world that we inhabit together. I choose to be gentle because my interior world, the experiences and beliefs embraced, will indirectly affect my students as we connect, dialogue, and feel our way through one another's worlds. If I am not transparent, holding a sacred space for myself, then the connections and relationships I create with students mimic the same vulnerabilities and insecurities that inhabit my own life.

I am an educator, a mom, a daughter, a wife, a lover, a sister, a friend, a colleague, and I would be remiss not to mention it all as I begin to discuss the story of "us," the educators. I have slowly learned that my "personhood" is not separate from my role as a teacher. The experiences, joys, struggles, and reflective moments I bring to Marian Hall Room 209, professional presentations or inside the public schools where I am teaching this year, intimately affect the relationships, instruction, and environments I'm developing with each and every student. I have not always known this.

As a young teacher, I felt obligated and almost panicky to show up with expertise, perfection, if possible, and an "I'm not going to fail" disposition. For I had been trained and mentored as a teacher who learned all about children with exceptional needs and had been working in the classroom for two whole semesters! I was becoming a young expert. I was driven, enthusiastic, and motivated to reach every student encountered. I was ready. I was probably a "mediocre" teacher, but I was performing. To be completely honest, I left the building on many days feeling disillusioned, disappointed, and defensive.

Fast forward to 2008—I was now an instructor in a small liberal arts university with children and adolescents of my own, years of experience in a variety of counseling and educational positions, and above all, I held a doctoral degree. Now, I was really the expert and knew exactly how to prepare future teachers, or so I thought and imagined. Once again, there were days when I felt effective, connecting to my students and therefore the content. There were other days, many of them, where I stood and robotically delivered dry disconnected passages, statistics, and case studies. I was reminded by those rows of disenchanted, yawning, and "rolling-eyed" facial expressions that I had left out personal facets or had not shared the stories of commonality that result in a reflective capacity, deepening connections and therefore learning. This void between my students and me was tangible. A void that only felt tangible when "quiet" resounded inside the car driving home from class.

It was an interesting and different time in education. The national educational scene was pointedly focused on test scores, achievement gaps, and an emphasis on teacher and student performance. The execution of the Special Education Law was shifting back and forth and "accountability" and "no excuse cultures" were the new buzz words and topics for teachers, administrators, and students. "Zero Tolerance" regulations for behavioral and emotional challenges of many students were being implemented in increasing numbers of schools, especially new charter schools. There was a palatable national and state reform shift, but the emotional connections, relationships and "feeling felt" moments inside many individual classrooms were eternally present; yet, many political and educational reformers had forgotten the significance of these relationships and connections—including me during brief moments.

I don't feel the above description of my roles and feelings are much different than the majority of educators who awaken each morning thinking, pondering, and questioning their responsibilities and the massive amount of peripheral factors that affect so many of our students and instruction. Sometimes these external educational demands and factors feel very much out of our control. Or maybe they simmer in the back of our minds. The "politics" of reform overwhelms our thinking as we forget that one successful enriching experience is where we begin. Simply stated, joining with a student, classroom, or school at the emotional and social developmental stages begins building a momentum of extravagant emotional competency. It is here that a sense of safety and belonging builds on the academic hierarchy of sustainable learning.

The educators of our children and adolescents understand how connection, compassion, and the hunger to be heard and understood are the pinnacles of educational envisioning/re-visioning reform. This section of the story is about you, me, and all of us as we explore the "vocation" that has placed us in front of and beside our world's youth. It is about relationships inside a living system that has masked itself through the subtle words, behaviors, and movements of individuals and groups who have forgotten that people change people, not programs. As Michael and I sat together for three days in Pittsburgh, talking about the content of this story, we reminded one another that to be college and career ready is much grander and deeper than proficiency in math, language arts, and science. Because education is about maximizing human potential and living outside the walls of school, these words and this story is as much about us as teachers, parents, and administrators, as it is the children and adolescents we teach.

I know that when I feel empty, unsuccessful, sad, and disillusioned (among other negative emotions), my own biological children and those students whom I stand before, feel the effects of my disposition and state of mind. Dr. Dan Seigel, psychiatrist, researcher, and author discusses this overlap and intermingling of emotion within ourselves and others in his articles and books, explaining this experience as "mindsight." Mindsight is the ability to feel and observe our own emotions and those of others. We could define this as personal insight accompanied by a deepened empathy, affecting all of our relationships. We have the neural circuitry to develop this capacity of "mindsight," and as Dr. Seigel repeatedly emphasizes, "Relationships shape the synaptic connections in the brain."[1] Mindsight is a sharing of energy and information flow that occurs with or without conscious awareness. When we join at a deepened conscious level with one another, the neural pathways in our brains are shaped differently. Our perspectives broaden and our ability to emotionally regulate experiences—responding rather than reacting (our synaptic connections)—become stronger with this awareness and practice. We begin to see ourselves and the world with a gentler understanding.

How do we do this? How do we make the time when our accountability and evaluation of performance and student growth metrics becomes our lifeline to job security? I wish more than anything I could type the words for a recipe, a foolproof plan, or equation for the needed time, understanding, and positive intentions that would create this connection. How do we stay motivated, nourishing that resiliency capacity posited in each of us? How do we generate emotional connections that build trust and plant seeds of hope in our students and ourselves? I would ulti- mately disrespect every reader of this story in trying to design and share a recipe or "fix" because we are a living system that changes, expands, breathes, explores, laughs, cries, and moves through a complex and personal history and present-day assortment of unending individual development. I feel we begin to answer many of these questions when we become attuned to ourselves. When we tap into those relationships, experiences, and deeper feelings that intuitively communicate with us, we begin to integrate differences and promote human connections. When we are feeling more integrated with ourselves, we move away from extreme states of mind of rigidity or chaos. We begin to find a gentler balance inside our own lives that will impact those we teach. We teach what we need to learn. What I am learning every day is that the negative emotions of others can only affect me if I choose to allow them to take up space in my thought process, while labeling them with immediate judgments and reactions. All individuals offer tremendous value to us, even when we desire diverse things and embrace different desires, beliefs, or interests. Individual differences are of great advantage when creating new ideas. Without this contrast and these vastly dissimilar experiences, we are unable to stimulate new thoughts, feelings, and responses to frustrating events and situations. There is value in every relationship and in every encounter, but it begins with the relationship and care I have and give to myself. This is anything but selfish. It is a necessary aspect of the teaching and learning process when we are called day after day to meet the many challenging needs of youth and environments that sometimes feel to be bar-riers, not only to the students' well-being, but to ours. Why spend all of this time talking about the impact of negative emotions and relationships? I don't know of another profession that calls for such an extensive reper-toire of emotional, social, and academic guidance, while holding a workable and palpable tension between vul-nerable thoughts and feelings of children and adolescents.

Others do not have the power to affect our experiences; only our responses to others and these experiences can trigger us in negative ways. This is sometimes a problematic concept to grasp. When others lash out in anger, their battle is not with us, but with themselves. And if we can detach from another's personal battle in a loving and gentle way, seeing their strengths even when hard to find the time, those individuals will leave us out of their battles. When we look for another's strengths, genius, passions, and gifts, our attention to this mindset amplifies these strengths.

At our core, we are more alike than different as human beings. When we explore and remember the positive aspects inside ourselves and others, over time we will begin to see more of these positive attributes, and therefore, so will those with whom we are in relationship. Nick Long, psychologist and special educator has worked with troubled youth and teachers for over fifty years. His work looks at the "conflict cycle" that educators and students often find themselves swirling inside and struggling against. Teachers and administrators can suddenly find themselves in these ongoing power struggles with students—not realizing how it happened or when. How did we become immersed in these conflicts? As educators and parents, we must remember that we can become emotionally triggered by the behaviors, words and perceived dispositions of our youth. In our secondary schools across our nation, the number one reason for an increase in student violence is staff-counter aggression.[2] Initially, this research was shocking to me, but as I have pondered the inner lives of educators, including my own, I am beginning to understand how our natural biological stress response system (fight, flight, or freeze instinct) is triggered inside those moments of reacting. We become caught up inside the student's conflict, often perpetuating the aggression and power struggles from adults. I have personally experienced this as a mother and a teacher, and on more than one occasion! We carry our personal stories into every relationship and environment. This fact alone is enough to create curiosity and cause us to question our own responses or reactions in challenging times. Our capacity and ability to implement self-care is a "best practice" we can benefit from as we create, maintain, and adjust our social and emotional connections with one another, ourselves, and our students.

These past few years have been roller coaster rides for many educators, parents, and students as the meaning of education has subtlety shifted to college and career readiness to the exclusion of all other aspects of a living system education. A few months ago, New York Times' OpEd columnist, David Brooks, shared a shift in his own thinking:

*"First, we've probably placed too much emphasis on early education. Don't get me wrong. What happens in the early years is crucial. But human capital development takes a generation. If you really want to make an impact, you've got to have a developmental strategy for all the learning stages, ages 0 to 25. Second, we've probably put too much weight on school reform. Again, reforming education is important. But getting the academics right is not going to get you far if millions of students can't control their impulses, can't form attachments, don't possess resilience and lack social and emotional skills."*[3]

Columnist David Brooks shared a bit of his own vulnerability in the ways he has shifted and described a perspective about education reform that is pliable and thought-filled, raising questions and notions that appear to cry out for challenge and examination as we look at the current outcomes and concerns that surround and infiltrate this present reform agenda.

Teachers spend on the average twelve thousand hours with students during their K-12 educational years. Next to a parent, a teacher is one of the most influential persons in a child's and an adolescent's life. Many of my friends and colleagues are immersed in parenting and education year round. As we begin another school year, it feels vitally important to honor and applaud the tumultuous, challenging, victorious, ever-changing school years we have all encountered, in spite of the so-called frustrating and endless power struggles and intense pronouncements from political and educational reformers who are constantly asking, "What can we do to improve the well-being of every stakeholder inside our schools?"

Our media tends to report on the negative and the human interest stories that pull at our heart strings. We read and listen to the "big stories," the monumental happenings, the life-changing experiences that school leaders and teachers meet inside the reported-ongoing revolution of educational reform. I cannot think of a more significant story to share with our community than the raw and heartfelt thoughts shared by teachers, who, each day are meeting the needs of a diverse, populous, and, in some cases, insolvent student population. Many of our students are simply trying to survive. Some get little sleep due to caring for siblings or relatives, while scarcely managing what feels like a chaotic and stress-filled existence outside of school. The stress that is experienced when an individual is in a chronic stress response literally shuts down the part of the brain that problem solves, emotionally regulates, and is able to plan and organize his or her life to move from point A to point B.

How do these variables affect our educators personally and professionally as they once again pack up their reflections, thoughts, feelings, disappointments, anxieties, victories, and intentions for their students and children who are re-entering another school year? How do these variables personally impact the students who are carrying into our classrooms worries, angst, hidden pain, and agendas we cannot see but need to understand?

A veteran first grade teacher wrote to me this past year from the Indianapolis Public School district and these were her thoughts and questions:

*"My burning question is this: In order to have a valid and conclusive science experiment you must pare down and single out the variables that contribute to the results. This is the only way you can tell without a doubt which variable is the root cause. Where is this concept located in the state's teacher evaluations? The 'powers that be' selectively forgot that the variables of free will and cultural upbringing within each student is a wild card that eliminates the possibility to realistically place blame for failing students on teachers alone!*

*My class this year is composed of twenty-two six- and seven-year-olds. I have spoken and met with three quarters of these families about their child's challenges, trying to understand and find ways to engage these young students. In our end-of-year NWEA testing last week, we had a third of our first grade students not meet the reading goals that NWEA had set for them after their fall testing period. These students were all our highest performing students. These tests are completely multiple choice in nature. Do we really know if the initial test results were accurate, or did they contain a fair amount of lucky guessing?*

*Lori, I am working from 7:30 a.m. to 6 p.m. every day and constantly trying to create new lessons to grab students' attention. I've tried every behavior modification strategy in the book and have overhauled my entire system of positive and negative rewards, but see very few changes. Many of my children are on medication for ADHD, oppositional behaviors, have very difficult home lives, and come to school exhausted, distracted, and unable to sit still to even listen to a short story at such a young age. I am exhausted."*

We cannot afford not to pay attention to these aforementioned factors that are as much a part of our classrooms as the content we teach. Parents and educators alike feel exhausted and overwhelmed by the pace and the increased expectations of all parties in this time of educational reform. Schools across the country are opening and closing under new leadership with parents feeling confused and upset over the changes they feel are out of their control. These are the realities as we delve into the educational arena at this time. I feel that most, if not all of us, deeply desire ways to meet the holistic needs of our most vulnerable children and students.

As Michael and I wrote the outline for this book several months ago, he put his pen down, looked at me and said, "Lor, everyone is busy. That's what I hear all the time, but busy doing what?" I thought about this question as we discussed further, finding myself caught up and tangled inside this category of "busyness." We all feel we're racing against time inside this vocation, with so much that is required of all educators, parents, students, and the community. Whether we acknowledge this or not, education and its changes are about our entire communities across the nation. Our students are observing, modeling, and consciously or subconsciously evaluating and mimicking our actions, words, and behaviors.

*Our relational dialogues and shared stories with children and youth bring awareness to the human condition, but it is only sustainable if we are true and gentle with ourselves.*

As I write these words, nine endless days ago, my sweet Dad passed away quickly and peacefully in his home. My story of an educator has suddenly shifted and is now about a daughter, who, as a teacher, is experiencing a part of herself that is wading in unknown waters. As children, we generally see our parents or caregivers, just as many adolescents see life—invincible, endless, and unchanging. We take for granted a presence that is tangible, that leaves voicemails, that argues with us, ties our shoes, wipes our tears, causes tears, walks us down the aisle, or possibly has been a faraway presence. These events in our lives cannot help but affect our relationships with others and ourselves.

In the weeks prior and directly following my dad's death, the priorities, tasks, meetings, and day-to-day occurrences quietly shifted, replaced by a more compassionate and vulnerable state of mind. Could this be where the teaching and learning balance becomes a dance of relationships (in and out of the classroom) leading us beyond education reform and into a re-visioning of education where all individuals are supported emotionally, socially, and cognitively?

The research in neuroscience has demonstrated how emotions and learning are intimately connected and processed in the brain. The story of the educator is about emotions and cognition. "The message from social and affective neuroscience is clear: no longer can we focus solely at the level of the individual student in analyzing effective strategies for classroom instruction. Teachers and students socially interact and learn from one another in ways that cannot be done by examining only the 'cold' cognitive aspects of academic skills."[4] When we look inward and explore the obstacles, passions, and the life processes in our own lives, we model this ability for our students and their personal stories. It is in this space of self-reflection that we might subtly alter how we present ourselves inside our classrooms, returning to a "joy" of teaching.

Below are lists of questions that might begin to lessen these emotional and cognitive chasms that are developing in this time of school reform challenges and debates. These questions do not solve problems; they explore what cannot be seen with only the eyes. These questions might propel a few more deep dives into reflection, initiating dialogue, while carrying to the surface some long held negative emotions and beliefs that have barricaded learning of both educator and student. Who are those students who trigger your emotions and leave you sleepless on many nights? What is it about these students or teachers that bring about negative emotion? These social and emotional questions have the potential to raise test scores and close those gaps, but more importantly, stimulate curious creative thinking patterns our brains are wired to hold and expand.

## Questions Drive All Learning

**What do I need?**

**What resources (people, activities, or things) could assist me in reaching my small and larger goals?**

**How can I show that I am progressing to larger goals?**

**What can my class do to assist me?**

**What can my teacher do to assist me?**

**How do I handle negative situations? When these situations occur, what do I typically say to myself?**

What would be a statement that would encourage me?

Who are my heroes? What are the character traits I admire in these people that make them my heroes?

How will I personally know I am on the right track? What will tell me I strayed off the track of my goals?

What are three negative emotions that I feel most often?

What are three positive emotions that I feel often or sometimes?

How could creative visualization help me?

How could I learn to begin again even after a day of small mistakes?

Name three strategies that my schoolteacher could begin that would assist me in moving toward my goals?

What are two or three challenges or obstacles that prevent me from reaching small or big goals?

What are my strengths?

What are my challenges?

Many educators are riding the waves of educational change with optimism and hope, creating classroom cultures where our "shared commonalities" as human beings are revered and discussed. Through the social and emotional and educational neuroscience research and its leading pioneers, we now understand that teachers are "brain changers." We have the honor, responsibility, and privilege to enrich the social, emotional, and cognitive environments of one another. As Dr. Goleman (1994) reported, "When 1,011 children were tested on the Profile of Nonverbal Sensitivity (PONS) assessment, those who showed an aptitude for reading feelings nonverbally were among the most popular in their schools, the most emotionally stable and they performed better academically. Their IQs were not higher than those of children who were less skilled at reading nonverbal messages—suggesting that mastering this empathic ability assists in classroom effectiveness."[5]

When we focus our energies on "seeing the very best" in every relationship and student, while listening to learn, we move beneath negative overt behaviors of many students, colleagues, or parents. We begin to understand there is much buried inside hurtful and angry words and actions. *"I am not enough"* is replaced with *"I might just be enough!"*

There are so many extraordinary educators who are moving forward and choosing to see the creativity and innate genius in all students, appreciating the varied personalities that walk through their classroom doors, and who invest in relationships, that for the students and parents, feel safe, secure, and motivating.

My heartfelt gratitude for all those educators who:

1. Try to see the "very best" in each and every student.
2. Listen to understand, not to respond.
3. Create a safe and collaborative culture where students feel comfortable in making mistakes and are motivated to keep going.
4. Get up every morning, feeling sometimes exhausted beyond description, but open their minds and hearts to those three or four vulnerable students who push their buttons and test the relationship just because they need to know that someone will still be there no matter their choices.

5. Create opportunities for children and young adults to discover their passions and strengths.
6. No matter the political and educational thermometer, you walk in the door and greet students with gratitude and are authentic in ways that create a mutual, respectful, and compassionate presence.

## MICHAEL

Lori's section on the educators' story has taken me back to my first year of teaching, now over thirty years ago, and a student that I remember well, whom I will call Dan. As I look back now at my early journey as a teacher of emotionally troubled and troubling young people, a journey in which my students have taught me at least as much as I have taught them, I think of Dan. He helped put me on a path toward becoming a "turnaround teacher." Dan guided me as I began to "see" underneath what I now know as pain-based behavior.

### Dan and Me

*The misbehavior of troubled children is seldom
what it first appears to be. Understanding this, I believe,
is the only place to start. No child has a need
to create a life of conflict.*

L. TOBIN

Dan, a twelve-year-old middle schooler, simply would not do anything I asked him to do. It seemed no matter what I asked of him he would intentionally do the opposite. Dan was an expert in quickly getting the entire class off task, and often, just short of my perception of out of control.

I vacillated between yelling at Dan, which never accomplished much other than having Dan yell back at me, usually with some fine expletives, to feeling so totally incompetent that I simply would not direct any comments to Dan, whatsoever. I quickly became unsure of what to do with him and unsure of myself as a teacher.

Whenever I tried to confront Dan, he would explode with rage and every other student in my class would look directly at me to "see" how I would respond. To this day, over thirty years later, I can vividly hear a voice in my head saying, "You have to do something! You cannot let him talk to you this way. Everyone is watching you, and if you do not do something, they too will begin to act like this! Do something!"

I would yell at Dan. I would tell him he could not talk to me like that (although he already had), and we had spawned a power struggle that would simply never end. When I would escort Dan down to the principal's office, he would curse at the principal, earning another suspension. Although it was never stated directly, it became obvious that the principal did not want to see Dan, ever! The not so subtle message was: "You're his teacher, handle him!" By early October of my first year teaching, I felt completely incompetent!

When I ignored Dan and allowed him to rule the classroom, he would quickly take over. All the other students were afraid of him, and underneath my thin veneer as a competent teacher, so was I. I was afraid of losing control. On these days, Dan never stopped his disruptive behavior. Eventually, usually well before lunch, chaos would ensue. The principal would come down to my class, Dan would curse him out, and he would be suspended for a number of days. Dan would return from his latest suspension in an even worse mood—if that were possible. The entire chain of events would start anew.

By Halloween I found myself looking out my classroom window every morning hoping and praying that Dan would not be on the bus that day. It became harder and harder for me to sleep through the night because I simply could not get Dan out of my mind. I was sure he really hated me, and when I was honest with myself, I also hated him. Here I was, two months into my career, and all I could think about was how much my life would improve if this twelve-year-old was not in my classroom. By the way, Dan never missed a day of school.

By mid-November, I felt desperate and despondent. My confidence level was at an all-time low, and I felt as if every other teacher in the school, when they saw me, would lower their eyes and shake their heads. Teachers quickly seem to know when other teachers' classrooms are "out of control." No one came to my aid.

Somehow I managed to make it to the winter break. Dan was now on my mind all of the time. To this day I remember crying before having to begin school again after the break. I really lost the entire concept of Dan as a twelve-year-old-troubled-young person, as he became a continuous nightmare. I decided to take a graduate class that fall semester on classroom management. One late evening after a particularly horrible day with Dan, I was sitting in my graduate class and the professor was telling us about a management technique where the teacher mirrors the students' disruptive behavior so that the student can "see" what his dysfunctional behavior looks like.

Theoretically the student would choose not to continue his behavior once he or she saw how immature it looked. To this day I am not sure if this is exactly a technique that this professor taught or simply my interpretation of what I thought this technique was about. In any case, I was desperate enough to try anything!

The next day I came to school "armed" with my new strategy. Dan got off the bus (yes, I was still watching and hoping from the window that he would not show up for school) and entered my class in an even fouler mood than usual. He was highly agitated and was pacing around the room. He approached his desk and kicked it over. All the other students seemed to once again look over to see what I, the "teacher," was going to do. I decided to use my "new technique," so I walked quickly toward Dan and I kicked over another desk right next to the one he had just kicked over.

Not aware of how stressed and out of control I was, I literally kicked this desk so hard that I broke my big toe and yelled out something teachers are not supposed to say in class. Most of the other students ran out of our classroom, and I vividly remember one of my female students freezing in place and starting to cry. Dan on the other hand was not fazed at all by my new mirroring technique. His behavior quickly escalated and he began to throw books and materials all around my classroom. Somehow I dragged Dan down the hall to the principal's office, that day, where he was suspended once again.

In the late spring Dan was placed in a foster home. I remember being a bit surprised. I had called Dan's home a number of times during the school year and his mother would always say that they could not handle him either. His mother even indicated that she was afraid of him. Even as a novice first year teacher, I quickly recognized that I was not going to get any help from his mother or his stepfather. I received a call from his new foster parents who invited me to attend one of the mandated counseling sessions. Once again, I was desperate to try anything, so I ended up attending a number of sessions. It was during one of those sessions that the therapist let me know that Dan had often been severely beaten by his alcoholic stepfather and Dan would often try to intervene when his stepfather would beat his mother. The therapist also indicated that Dan may have been sexually abused by an "uncle" for a number of years.

Now thirty years later, when my big toe aches from the cold weather, I often think back on my first year of teaching with Dan. I often wonder what became of him. Dan gave me my first very difficult lesson in what I have come to know as "Pain-Based Behavior." These behaviors are driven by children and youth in pain. I have also come to know over these three decades or so that we all have children in our care and our classrooms with various levels of pain in their lives.

As educators, parents, and community members, we all need to recognize these children and look beyond their surface behaviors. Their behaviors will make us all uncomfortable, anxious, and often angry; yet, we must recognize that at-risk children and youth, in need of our care, act in ways that push us away, often triggering the very adults who want to help them to respond in counter-aggressive and non-productive ways. We all must learn to do a much better job than I did with Dan.

### Turnaround Teachers

What separates "turnaround teachers" from other teachers is a question that has driven my learning for a number of decades. I have always been fascinated by what specific characteristics allow some teachers to flourish with very troubled young people, while others burnout and often become cynical. I have been a teacher and an administrator working with troubled children and youth for over twenty-five years, yet I struggled greatly early in my career. I stumbled on the concept of "turnaround teachers and schools" while learning about resiliency and school improvement.

Resilience research identifies the specific practices and beliefs of "turnaround" teachers and schools. Moreover, these studies are corroborated by research into the characteristics of teachers and schools that successfully motivate and engage youth, including those now labeled "high performing, high poverty schools."[6]

A very common finding from this research is the power of a teacher to change and influence the direction of at-risk young people's lives. Werner and Smith (1989) found that, "For the resilient youngster, a special teacher was not just an instructor for academic skills but also a confidant and positive model for personal identification."[7]

We now can identify the practices of turnaround teachers as well as turnaround schools. One of the key characteristics of turnaround teachers is what they intentionally choose to notice and see. Turnaround teachers are always on the lookout for "sparks." They notice them, cultivate them, and speak to the sparks they see in others. Turnaround teachers want to light fires within the young people they work with, not fill buckets with memorized meaningless information. Lighting fires with your most difficult students begins with sparks. Teachers can start extremely large bonfires if we pay attention to finding sparks within the students we teach. Finding and lighting sparks also allows us to establish authentic connections with students who may be reluctant to connect with adults. It allows us as teachers to begin to make connections and build positive meaningful relationships based on "loving support."

*Throughout history the most successful youth workers have been able to see beyond the problems of young people to a vision of their great potential.*
RECLAIMING YOUTH INTERNATIONAL

So, what is a spark? A spark is a special quality, skill, or interest that lights us up. It is what we are passionate about. Something that comes from inside of us, and when we express it, it gives us joy and energy. It's our very essence, the thing about us that is *good and beautiful, and useful to the world.*

To begin with, we can ask ourselves as teachers if we know what our own sparks are. Do we know what we ourselves are passionate about, and can we share it with the young people we work with? As teachers we can begin to "notice" mindfully. This can be accomplished easily as we go about our work as teachers. Do you notice when students get new sneakers, or do you notice and see when they may change a hairstyle or get a new phone? Not only do we notice as teachers, but we can speak to what we notice that is unique within each of the young people we sit beside. What seems to "brighten" their eyes? We can begin to help our students see strengths within themselves that they have not "seen" for themselves. These strengths can go well beyond a narrow focus of academic skills. What are their interests after school? How big is their family? Do they have jobs and what are they? What movies do they enjoy watching and what kind of music do they like? Do they get along well with others? Are they good friends to others? Are they kind and supportive of others? As we work with our students we can practice noticing—seeing them and looking for their individual "sparks."

We begin to convey the message to all students that they are important and unique and that they matter! By noticing, we begin to convey unconditional regard for all our students as individuals with gifts that can be deepened and cultivated. As their teacher we may spend more time with the young people in our classrooms than any other adult in their lives. We can notice their unique sparks, affirm those sparks, and as we teach, cultivate and deepen their unique sparks. *Turnaround teachers watch for signs of sparks and speak to what they see:*

"You really seem to enjoy_____."; "I notice that you are really good with_____."; "Did you recognize how well you were able to _____?"; "You seem really interested in _____."; "Wow, you have a gift for_____."

Turnaround teachers will often share their own sparks and what they find exciting. They intentionally model their sparks with their students. Remember, all emotions are contagious. Our excitement will spark excitement in our students even when they have no interest in what we are doing! Sparks are contagious! Modeling a variety of possible "sparks" can light fires for a lifetime. As you share your own sparks, allow your students to know that sparks can and do change throughout one's life. You can gather sparks along your path. Turnaround teachers ask their students questions about their sparks and listen deeply to the answers they receive. Listening and reflecting is the gateway to creating connections with all human beings.

Another characteristic that comes to mind concerning turnaround teachers, is the ability to intentionally build connections with his or her students. These connections must focus on what we see as "strengths" in our students rather than perceived weaknesses. Focus on what is strong, not what is wrong.

> *Glance at problems, gaze at strengths.*
>
> J. C. CHAMBERS

Brendtro and Larson (2004) quote James Hillman's (1996) use of the acorn metaphor to describe each child's unique hidden potential. *"A tiny acorn carries coded instructions for becoming a mighty oak. All children are endowed with the seed for some unique 'genius.' In the struggle to find their purpose, they make missteps and show many problems. Our task is to provide opportunities so children can discover their destiny and calling."*[8]

Turnaround teachers recognize that building connections and helping their students find their sparks and strengths is an endurance event, not a one-shot deal. Many of the young people we have chosen to work beside will need consistent care over time before they begin to trust. Many may also be accustomed to teachers coming in and out of their lives without even the slightest form of connection. We can demonstrate our commitment to building these connections by showing up at our students' activities. These are the events that are related to their sparks. These can include: school plays, sporting events, dance recitals, or even showing up at a part-time job they have. Many of our students perform at work very well, and we can create an opportunity allowing them to know we notice and care. These attempts at connection will pay huge dividends for us back in our classrooms and are a proactive way turnaround teachers forge connections with their most difficult students.

Turnaround teachers also have a strength that is very gentle. William E. Krill, author of the book *Gentling*, defines teacher gentleness this way: *"A teacher capacity that is rarely spoken about is the teacher's capacity for 'gentleness.' Gentleness involves a kind of strength and assurance in the giver. Gentleness may be delivered in a firm and assertive manner . . . it is not always soft and sweet but it is always respectful. 'Gentling' includes a calming presence, a safe tone of voice, and eyes filled with compassion. This of course cannot be faked! Also...an empathetic touch . . . that can be light as a feather or firm as a safe encompassing hug. What would the world be like without gentleness? It is a marker that makes human beings human in the larger sense. It also needs to be modeled for all children and youth."*[9]

Turnaround teachers have integrated their strength with gentleness. Turnaround teachers have made an intentional commitment *not* to be one of those "drive-by adults" in the lives of the students they teach. We, as educators, can be instrumental in creating a school culture where all students are valued and respected for who they are. My final thoughts originate from the work of David Richo. All human beings have higher needs. Turnaround teachers continue to learn and continue to want to make a difference in the lives of the children and youth who they serve. Richo puts it this way:

*"Our higher needs include making full use of our gifts, finding and fulfilling our calling, being loved and cherished just for ourselves, and being in relationships that honor all of these. Such needs are fulfilled in an atmosphere of the five 'A's by which love is shown: attention, acceptance, appreciation, affection, and allowing."*[10]

Richo goes on to say that the majority of people think of love as a feeling; however, love is not so much a feeling as a way of being present with the people in our lives. Turnaround teachers provide abundant love in the form of Richo's five "A"s. Human beings flourish within that atmosphere. All children need to experience attention, acceptance, appreciation, affection, and allowing. These are the ingredients that will lead to healthy and productive human beings. Remember, as a teacher, you have the power to transform lives.[11]

## SPARKS

1. A broadened and flexible perspective allows us to see inside the world of our children and adolescents and our own strengths, and challenges those experiences or relationships that trigger negative emotions! Take deep breaths and try to spend a few minutes alone each day reflecting on a perspective that takes a new snapshot of "how" we can collaborate with one another inside our homes and schools this fall.

2. Pack up those teaching and parenting moments that didn't go well, and ask your children and students for input as you design and orchestrate new schedules, rules, guidelines, and consequences. Find agreed upon times to discuss the day, the challenges, and the successes.

3. Teaching is never about saving a soul. When we begin to fill ourselves with positive emotions, experiences, and relationships, we are mentally priming the brain for emotionally connecting with our most challenging students. What activity, hobby, relationship or "new way" of looking at a previous situation can you recreate and model for your students? Our children intuitively experience the transparency within our communication, and understand our non-verbal expression much more than what we verbally say. Take time for yourself, placing yourself

in the company of those who lift you up and bring a bit of laughter back into your daily life.

4. Plan a community classroom meeting once a week identifying and celebrating those aspects of the week that went well! Develop two or three goals for the following week and write down a classroom plan for how to reach those goals. Our students need to be the initiators of these gatherings. Follow their lead and affirm their solutions, ideas, and suggestions. Talk to your colleagues, other children and adolescents, and glean from diverse perspectives.

5. We create a gentler and productive conversation when feelings and thoughts are not hot, negative, and misinterpreted. When we listen to understand and learn, we broaden our perspectives and increase positive emotions in the brain.

6. When we share a story, actually personalizing the subject matter, we become "real" people with "real" feelings and experiences standing before and alongside those who dare us to teach them! In turn, by sharing a part of ourselves, as we create a compassionate presence inside our schools and homes, we self-reflect, re-think, and re-appraise our own stories and beliefs and how we came to embrace these so tightly. Maybe it is time to stretch, allow, and refigure what does not serve us inside our lives any longer. *Our students are our greatest teachers!*

7. Questions are processed in the brain long after they have been asked. When we question with deference, inquiring from a need to solve a problem, the question unlocks the key to collaboration and invites equity into every relationship. What do you need? How can I help? In our schools where children and adolescents have very few choices and feel a lack of control, providing opportunities to receive feedback, possible options, and ways to

relate in self-challenging situations pave the path for trusting relationships, increased motivation, and higher achievement.

*Every encounter in our lives happens for a higher purpose; every meeting is a chance for evolution. We should always ask ourselves how we can grow from our associations, challenges and friendships. This makes our connections and partnerships far more meaningful and empowering.*

JAMES WANLESS, IN *LITTLE STONE*

# CHAPTER 3

# The Student's Story

*The student is infinitely more important*
*than the subject matter.*

NEL NODDINGS

## LORI

THIS PAST YEAR, the story of an educator and the story of a student have taken on a new meaning for me as a current instructor in higher education. I stepped out of the singular role as assistant college professor and entered four fifth-grade classrooms in a large diverse public school district, Washington Township Schools, in Indianapolis. I co-taught two mornings a week in two classes in two diverse schools each semester. I have never worked harder or learned more in my life! On Tuesday and Thursday mornings, I left the fifth-grade classrooms and entered Marian Hall to teach pre-service teachers followed by a couple of hours of late afternoon class preparation. I then returned to campus in the evenings, teaching graduate students who were first and second year teachers in charter and public schools across Indianapolis.

During the last nine months, I remembered how it felt to be inside a school and classroom, walking with a very unsteady gait and moments of feeling completely incompetent. It was a wobbly walk, filled with many blunders, blossoming connections to teachers and students I had never expected, an abundance of reflective moments, and a great appreciation for returning to the classroom where every teacher and student is intimately affecting the social, emotional, and academic lives of one another. I was reminded that teaching is not something you learn to do, once and for all, and then teach problem-free forever. Teaching changes every day. In teaching, one must always remain open to something new and unpredictable. Good teaching is a dynamic process and is never static. Teaching is alive and fluid. Good teaching is an interactive process, a dance, which begins and ends with "seeing" the student. We must always be mindful that deep learning is profoundly relational.

When we see teaching as more than simply the transmission of knowledge from one person to another, it changes everything we do. I am reminded of the original meaning of the word "education," according to its Latin roots. Education is about leading out or bringing forth that which is already within a human being. To truly attempt to educate a young person is to try and find ways of reaching inside another. We, as teachers, want to find, as well as nourish, the unique gifts of each child and connect that to our academic subject matter.

Monday nights were designated fifth-grade-preparation-homework nights, sitting on the floor in our hallway upstairs trying like hell to create an aligned academic standard-driven lesson that implemented the potential of each student's unique brain aptitude. It is one thing to stand behind a podium and lecture about the research and implications of educational neuroscience, and it is quite another to sit beside these brilliant, diverse, ornery, and emotionally ignited students, testing you each moment to see if you are up for the challenge, and connecting to those parts of themselves that so often feel inadequate and unsuccessful.

## Power of Stories

What I have discovered these last few months is that not only is the implementation of "storytelling" brain compatible with how we learn, but when we share some personal aspects of stories with our students, we can tap into their emotions that can create a connection to one another enhancing collaboration in our classrooms. The brain is a social organ, and we are wired to bond with one another for survival and relationship. Relationships shape brain circuitry. We are wired to survive, and we pay attention to anything that feels threatening; but we also are neurobiologically circuited to "need" one another, to procreate and to empathize, instilling collaboration and cooperation among people and groups, which promulgate feelings of safety and belonging. If we do not feel safe and "felt," our motivation and desire to learn, to put forth effort, even to make a mistake simply disappears. During the last hundred thousand years and beyond, our brain circuitry has evolved; however, our modern lifestyles, environments, and circumstances have advanced significantly faster than our brain development. Our experiences in this time are much different than what we collectively faced years ago, and our brain circuitry is affected.

We need stories to assist us in remembering our

heritage, our personhood, our goals, visions, our commonalities with others, and most important, to know how very emotionally connected we are. We must remember that emotions are the gatekeepers of our students' intellect.

Stories have the power to change the direction of our lives and our learning. We write stories. We tell and listen to stories. We may not sit around a glowing campfire sharing these missives within stories, but we share through dialogues, day-to-day conversations, presentations, lectures, disciplining, and even through social media. Instagram, Facebook, and even Twitter bring us to a link or provide a brief glimpse from a personal blog or someone's experience that can awaken us to other perspectives and choices. We relate, agree, disagree, feel challenged, empathize and then unconsciously weave these stories into our own lives to see if there is a similar experience, thought process, or feeling. We take turns spinning stories that assist us in feeling accepted and affirmed as we try to make sense out of our lives and the world we inhabit.

The truth about stories is that they are subjective. They are told, written, and expressed through perspectives, perceived values, belief systems, and experiences we embrace. Somehow, we collectively and individually begin to identify and attach ourselves to these stories even when they no longer serve us in a way that is aligned to who we are *now* and who we are becoming. We subconsciously hold onto these stories, possibly fearful of changes in our lives. The path of least resistance for many of us feels comfortably familiar, and the risk to leave feels too enormous. We oftentimes forfeit a new path or an unacquainted option that taps into our strengths, passions, and genius! These stories, both ours as teachers and theirs as our students, become our "private realities." They become the filter with which we view our world.

School is typically the first place and first social experience where one is required to live and interact beyond the context of family and all we have known to be true. It is in "school" one learns how to live outside the walls of school, finding purpose mastery and accrued independence!

Have we forgotten? Have we asked our students for their stories? Do we know how they see their world? Have we shared our stories with our students? Peers, exposure to new adults, procedures, transitions, and simply finding one's way are critical in these formative school years. We are learning to relate to ourselves and to one another—as every child and adolescent theorist has shared. Have we forgotten these veritable complex blueprints of human (student) development? Have we forgotten the purpose of these integral and sometimes hot and messy stages we move through at different times and intervals throughout childhood and young adulthood?

*Humans are a living system and there is nothing linear,*
*logistical, or fluid in how each unique brain*
*and heart learns, remembers, retrieves, and embraces*
*relationships and knowledge!*

Stories and storytelling are innately how the brain learns, manipulates, and grasps information. When stories are filled with emotion and personal narratives, we create associations and make meaning inside our own experiences and lives. All our young have an inherent, built-in capacity for positive growth and development. Children walk into the classroom each school year with a "new story," but sometimes those stories are filled with thoughts, beliefs, and feelings that recycle worn out patterns reflected from familial systems, stifling creativity and expression. For the child and adolescent, the thoughts, feelings and attachments to those stories are pliable, easily shifted and changed depending upon the enriched environment, seeds of hope, and portals an educator can provide and model. Positive shifts in young people's lives happen when they are embedded in nurturing relationships and nurturing environments that meet their basic need for safety and belonging.

Metaphors and communal personal stories about our existence are an effective way to establish emotional links, reinforcing the values and standards we want to create in our classrooms and lives. The culture of "stories" created in our schools can directly and indirectly affect our students' sense of purpose and autonomy. When we understand ourselves, we begin to understand others. Self-knowledge is not emphasized enough in school, but research repeatedly reports it leads to increased motivation and self-efficacy.[1] When we assist a student with sharing his or her "life story," we begin to learn about her purpose, his fears, her perceived challenges, his strengths and interests. We quite possibly begin to understand a bit of pain and shame that looks different in front of peers, sitting behind desks at 9 a.m. on a Wednesday morning.

Oftentimes, children and adolescents who act and look aggressive, anxious, or withdrawn show up in our homes, classrooms, and communities with behaviors and labels such as the "bully," the oppositional "ring leader," or the apathetic "troublemaker." What looks hurtful, intentional, and outwardly defiant might be behaviors trying to mask a spirit of "felt" brokenness—children and teens who feel *much pain and sadness* beneath these exterior layers and labels. Our children and adolescents come into this world curious, wondering, optimistic, and asking questions, but they tend to leave secondary school with hearts and minds closed off, forgetting their innate creativity and passions as their questions slowly fade away. How do we create a compassionate existence inside our classrooms and schools inviting relationships of trust and community?

This past academic year, I observed fifth-grade teachers establish this presence through a process of mutual learning and a growing unified respect. These teachers taught me about "learning from students." We tried on different perspectives, ways to "see" our students, and trusted our students to understand and be gentle with our mistakes as we promised to be with theirs. We reminded each other that there is no real learning without a safe place to make mistakes. Together, we intentionally created that kind of place. As a team of teachers, we began to explore various perspectives, modeling shifts in our thought processes for our students. With these new lenses, conflicts lessened, and students began to feel a part of the solution with some autonomy. When children and adolescents feel safe enough to try out a new idea, contribute an unusual thought to a discussion, or explore an untried solution, they do! We in turn have an opportunity to provide feedback, dialogue, and discover novel ways to tussle with challenges and solutions.

The following is a story about something that recently occurred in a fifth grade classroom where I was co-teaching. This experience enhanced my understanding of the power of perspective and how the use of a little distraction can help to avoid unnecessary power struggles and conflicts. Not only did the student and I avoid a potential conflict, but we also connected with each other in a positive way. A few months ago, twelve-year-old Darren began his typical rendition of a poor choice sequence of tiresome behaviors. He was bouncing out of his seat without permission, interrupting instruction as he conversed with students around him. When Darren was asked to turn around or to please sit down, there was the usual eye rolling, denying, and increased anger. I decided to create a shift for both of us, and thought of Darren's expertise and strengths. I knew Darren was very familiar with smart phones and probably knew more than I did even at twelve years old. I used his knowledge and leadership and an abbreviated story to turn our perspectives around. "Darren, I need to respond right away to one of my students who just e-mailed me at the University, but I have to prepare for our group discussion in three minutes. Could you please send her a message for me?" I pulled out my phone and called up the e-mail. I explained to Darren what I wanted to say.

There are no words to describe how excited he was as he crafted a perfect message to my undergraduate student, forgetting his bad mood and his "felt" opposition towards the class and me. I thanked him and we began again. Darren asked if he could use his new phone to pull up additional research while other students moved to the computers. The rest of the afternoon felt different and pleasurable, as my perspective guided Darren onto a precipice of feeling capable and successful.

This story of my encounter with Darren could have easily gone in a completely different direction that would have Darren once again visiting the principal's office and moving through a list of various "consequences" for his inappropriate behavior. It would have been a sequence of events that Darren at age twelve and the adults who work with him are very familiar with, ending once again with Darren feeling less and less capable and successful at school. Project these kinds of encounters out, and one can see why in many places in America over fifty percent of our Darrens eventually drop out of school.

Storytelling is an evolutionary tradition that is as relevant and important today as it was thousands of years ago, when words in print were nonexistent. When we implement stories inside our homes and schools, we weave our personal narratives, the dry subject matter, and our life experiences into a context that helps us to make sense and meaning inside our worlds. When we tap into a child's prior knowledge, culture, and beliefs, we ignite their motivation to expand, grow into their capabilities and genius, making meaningful connections to relationships and academic content.

Both Michael and I are tiring of the word "rigor" in the current school reform movement. We seem to have forgotten the other "R" words that came along with the now over-used term "rigor." The other "R" words are relationship, resilience, and relevance. Without these other "R" words, the entire concept of rigor simply turns off the innate learning capabilities of human beings. Children and adults shut down because our brains are social organs.

Our schools and communities are crying out for an emotional connection inside classrooms where optimism, positive emotion, and life skills are sorely missing. Our heartfelt intention is to share and integrate these emotional and social building blocks inside our classrooms, discussing what we all can do as we begin implementing a tribal culture that is safe, optimistic, and filled with relational learning and connections. These connections begin with one heart, one student, one story, and one teacher at a time. Our children are our greatest teachers when we open up and remember that to ask, to listen, and to reframe the "possible" is the greatest teaching strategy we can bring to our future world citizens.

### *Still I Rise...*

There is a young boy who awakens to the world each day entering our classrooms with such sensitivity that he finds it hard to untangle from the "pulls" of his perceived world. He holds tightly to these long held feelings of shame, self-blame, and doubt that have been a part of his personal story throughout his lifetime. He seems to intuit the negative and positive emotions from all those around him, which feels heavy and not very manageable on most days. School is difficult because it is a place of constant social monitoring, evaluation, and sorting of people. To this young man, learning the subjects is the easy part of a school day. Looking competent, feeling at ease, and desperately trying to hide that dark torrid secret of shame and inexplicable low self-worth he feels down deep is all consuming.

His inner world is filled with pain, unanswered questions, and sketchy explanations as to "why" he feels such loss, anxiety, and interminable sadness. There is a pleading desire to feel better. He tries to remember homework, to complete assignments, to live a life where there is some laughter, play, and imagination. He feels somewhat loved and supported by his family, but life keeps shouting in his head, "You're not enough!" Most days, he believes this. His overt opposition, defiance, and off-the-cuff hostility create aggressive feelings in the adults and students around him.

There is a looming cloud of continual misunderstanding that has become a definitive aspect of communicating with this young man.

In seventh grade, something shifts ... Mr. Walt caught his attention on the first day of school. This teacher noticed the pain behind his eyes and seemed to immediately find a different pulse, a heartbeat of hope that had been waiting years for discovery. During those first few weeks of school, there were no long conversations shared or questions asked. There was only a knowing that potential and genius were locked away in a young mind that could not see and feel his way through a worn out story that no longer served him. Mr. Walt noticed a disconnect of mind and heart—a barren emotional landscape where seeds of hope were ready for planting.

Below is an assignment that began a trajectory of varied perspectives, a claiming of a new story, and an ending that became the beginning...

*Mr. Walt asked his English classes what gifts their ancestors had given them and how they planned to use these attributes to overcome the challenges they were up against today. He asked the students to write out their own strengths—a simple list of at least five accomplishments, happenings, or experiences where they had begun to feel a little more successful or capable. He challenged them to put their answers in poetry, a short story, or a piece of art. The students and Mr. Walt discussed the gifts of their ancestors and the challenges they faced in difficult times. "History always repeats itself," Mr. Walt reminded them. "They gave us courage, adversity, strong bodies and evolving minds. They gave us stories and poetry to build upon. They gave us freedoms: freedom of religion, freedom of speech, and the right to pursue happiness individually and collectively."*

For this young boy, this assignment, coupled with

gentle questioning and encouragement, spawned a new way of seeing himself in the world. As he continued to write out his strengths, interests, and visions, the unfolding story prompted by the questions asked throughout the school year, led to an exciting project. This young man became excited about a summer vocation of creating and envisioning "green golf courses." His grades improved and the filling of a void that had left him relying on the affirmations and approval of others began to lessen. As his story evolved, so did his confidence, successes, and motivation to try even in the face of failure.

Mr. Walt decided to gather the teams of teachers in this large middle school to develop a template for an ongoing "personal story" for each student. This student-crafted story would follow the student into every class and grade level from this point forward. The teachers were interested, and decided to create a protocol for this soon-to-be termed, "E-Story." The teachers began to construct and model these story templates for the students.

Just as an IEP follows students from grade level to grade level (mentioned again below), Michael and I are discussing how student-generated stories will be passed along each year so that "connections," the emotional bridges, can be fashioned with the deepened understanding of *who* that child or adolescent is. What are her goals, his dreams, her challenges, his strengths, passions, and her obstacles that contribute to the unique expression and personhood of every student?

### MICHAEL

These E-Stories can serve as a window into the lives of the students we serve. As their E-Story unfolds and as the students move along their educational journey, these stories can shed light on the students' unfolding gifts, serving as a guide for both themselves and their future teachers. We live at a time of "data driven decision making" yet we really fail to look at the entire picture. We are missing very important data as we attempt to work with the young people we serve. The following questions can begin to take you toward the "missing data" and we may begin to "see" the young people we teach in a much deeper manner.

What are your students' stories? What does an individual student's brokenness appear like inside your classroom? What is the main idea threaded throughout the overt behaviors, words, and engagement or lack thereof? How long has he or she been swirling inside the eye of the storm?

We begin with the questions. We attempt to unravel a story that is still fresh, malleable, and ready for a partner and a renewed purpose. It begins with purpose. Are we able to help one another discover purpose inside our stories?

 S P A R K S

**Outline of the E-Story**

**PART ONE**
**Origin (Describe your Nest)**
    **A. Place of Birth**
    **B. First Memories**
    **C. Family**
    **D. "Favorites"**

Questions

1. What was it like?
2. Who was there?
3. What stories do you remember from your childhood?

PART TWO
Early Adventures Away From the Nest
  A. First School Experience
  B. Friendships
  C. Enjoyment
  D. Celebrations
  E. Challenges
  F. Strengths/ Interests
  G. Service to Others

PART THREE
Dreams/Goals
  A. Visioning
  B. Expectations
  C. How will you get there?
  D. Who are your people of support?
  E. What people inspire you?
  F. Service to Others

*Samples of Art, Music, and any Artifacts to share*
*"Who You Are"*

Much like an Individualized Education Plan, the E-Story will accompany each student through his or her school years. This student-generated story can be modified, reworked, and shared during various times throughout the academic year. Younger students may begin to showcase their lives through pictures and artwork. Older students may want to add sections, revise current categories, and change the format as they see their life journeys unfolding each semester or school year.

Play with this outline, using your classes to assist in creating the format of the E-Story that best serves your present classroom culture. Implement student feedback and suggestions to highlight the community of individual learners and your current classroom traditions. Design opportunities and choices of activities that invite service to one another. These could be very small activities inside the classroom or student-organized and led community service projects. It is through the process of stepping outside ourselves that we generate positive emotions, which in turn, light up the frontal lobes of the brain, boosting higher-level thought processes.

### *Still I Rise*

MAYA ANGELO

You may write me down in history
With your bitter, twisted lies,
You may tread me in the very dirt
But still, like dust, I'll rise.

Does my sassiness upset you?
Why are you beset with gloom?
'Cause I walk like I've got oil wells
Pumping in my living room.

Just like moons and like suns,
With the certainty of tides,
Just like hopes springing high,
Still I'll rise.
Did you want to see me broken?

Bowed head and lowered eyes?
Shoulders falling down like teardrops.
Weakened by my soulful cries.
Does my haughtiness offend you?
Don't you take it awful hard
'Cause I laugh like I've got gold mines
Diggin' in my own back yard.

You may shoot me with your words,
You may cut me with your eyes,
You may kill me with your hatefulness,
But still, like air, I'll rise.

Does my sexiness upset you?
Does it come as a surprise
That I dance like I've got diamonds
At the meeting of my thighs?

Out of the huts of history's shame
I rise
Up from a past that's rooted in pain
I rise
I'm a black ocean, leaping and wide,
Welling and swelling I bear in the tide.
Leaving behind nights of terror and fear
I rise
Into a daybreak that's wondrously clear
I rise
Bringing the gifts that my ancestors gave,
I am the dream and the hope of the slave.
I rise
I rise
I rise.

LORI L. DESAUTELS, PH.D. AND MICHAEL MCKNIGHT, M.A.

# CHAPTER 4

# The Story of Emotions

*We are feeling creatures who think.*
DR. JILL BOLTE TAYLOR

*Development, it turns out,*
*occurs through this process*
*of progressively more complex exchange*
*between a child and somebody else—*
*especially somebody who's crazy about that child.*
URIE BRONFENBRENNER

## LORI

**W**RITING A BOOK, a chapter, or a word about a "living system" is a process and one that is derived from experiences perceived, lived, and remembered. Amazingly, as I began gathering and revisiting these words and chapters in preparation for meeting Michael this week, I plopped down at the computer, laid my fingers on the keys and became still, and then thought: This book will never be completed as we are truly fused inside a living system. I am revisiting a recent event, which has occurred over the past several months, recalled not solely as an educator, but as a mom. As I begin to share a bit about these living moments, I have no idea how this particular story will end, resolve, or affect the people or the events in the future. I do know there will be much learning and emotion—without assessments, formal instruction, and presented academic standards. Personally, I do not remember a time when I have had to allow so much, to let go of outcomes, and shift perspectives over and over again. The following words are about my hero, my son, and quite possibly, your child, student, friend, or loved one.

At 23 years of age, Andrew is experiencing some significant anxiety and depression. These feelings of loss and deprivation have affected all aspects of his life and school. As the wheels have temporarily fallen off his complex and continuous life journey, his cognitive, social and emotional development has also been stymied. He has been living inside a world swirling with perceived stress, unable to clearly think through everyday challenges.

As I stand beside hundreds of educators and students each week, one of the first statements to leave my lips is: *"All behavior is communication."* Andrew has been communicating to our family, professors, counselors, and friends consistently for the past several months. His communication has become loud and clear, as he speaks through his behaviors. This past week I fully realized I needed to listen deeply, to learn, and not to respond. As a family, we can guide, suggest, and create boundaries, but, ultimately, the repair and reconciliation is Andrew's discovery and passage to make.

Academically, Andrew is re-thinking and stepping back, but with feelings of penetrating sadness and possibly long held self-disappointment. These feelings have been generated by failing attempts over the past eight years during life's adolescent crucible. There are many milestones to be pursued in the young adult years; as I remember stress is never outside of any of us. Stress is this perceived "chronically felt disability"[1] that is often experienced as unreachable and unfixable in moments of distress. Through tears, voiced regrets, and choices to be made, I remember sitting on the floor in our living room asking Andrew, "What do you want? What do you need? What do you really want from life—now, in this moment?" His response was solid. "Mom, I don't know." As I vacillated between feeling helpless and wanting nothing more than to "fix" this situation for Andrew, I also knew we had been given a gift. The gift was not buried too deep, for it rested just below the surface in the form of a developing perspective and a tribe of supporters that have relentlessly held a compassionate presence for Andrew that exceeds the responsibilities of faculty, counselors, and even the most well intentioned mentors. I have actually been immersed inside a living educational system that has nurtured, gently questioned, and led Andrew with unequivocal understanding. Without the emotional support and care for the "whole student," I fear this new land we are exploring as a family, might have engulfed us in a quiet sea of despair and trepidation. I have been talking and urging educators to emotionally connect with the mind, body, and spirit of all students, but this "mother-son experience" has thrown me into the eye of an up-close-and-personal storm within a living system that thrives on emotional unions.

Over the past several months, I have been rethinking the word, "expert." I feel a proficient practitioner in any area is always learning, questioning, and perceiving "change" as a developmentally healthy aspect of environments, people, and relationships. I no longer use the term expert; I now consider myself, first and foremost, a learner and a teacher. I have spent the past twenty-five years teaching, mentoring, researching, and writing about children and adolescents who experience inner pain and unrecognizable shame. Dr. Larry Brendtro defines these emotions as "pain based behaviors."[2] These behaviors are so often misunderstood by society. We accept and empathize with physical challenges, such as immobility and compromised physical senses. We don't think twice when we observe hearing aids, eyeglasses, wheelchairs, and apparatuses that assist in living, moving, and experiencing the world in "normal" ways. We modify and accommodate instruction for children who learn differently, providing audio books, assistive technology, and continuous emotional support. As teachers, our frustration with how the brain learns rarely reaches the level where we become angry or aggressive toward a student. Yet, with children who experience pain and shame, we struggle to understand. We sometimes label these complex children and young adults as unlovable, unreachable, emotionally disturbed, emotionally dysfunctional, and void of empathy. These pain-based behaviors look lazy, aloof, unmotivated, arrogant, and possibly careless to us. We personalize a student's overt words and behaviors, while the emotions we begin to feel mimic those of children in pain. Dr. Nick Long repeatedly reports in his research that the number one reason for increased school violence is staff counter-aggression.[3] Intellectually and professionally, I sensed this. I taught in these sensitive educational environments alongside students and educators who knew there was more to these provincial mindsets, zero tolerance policies, punitive and misunderstood perspectives, and discipline processes relating to children with emotional disabilities.

As a mother, it is not so easy to separate from the age-old, iconic definitions that singularly label a person with emotional challenges. When we begin to understand the power of perspective and emotional connection, we begin to feel hopeful and less isolated. A living educational system is rooted in the power of presence, perspective, and active hope. As a family, we have experienced, first-hand, a "living system" in education! A living system provides a sense of purpose and affirms that every individual is doing his or her very best in the moment—no exceptions. It is always through this tangible and progressive process of personal connection that emotional, social, and cognitive learning are revealed. We are motivated and driven by the relational presence of others in our lives. As Maurice Elias from Rutgers University has stated, "All long-term learning takes place in the context of relationships."[4]

Although this story is focusing on our youth and educators, we tend to place an emphasis on education reform from kindergarten through twelfth grade. The research consistently reports that the prefrontal cortex does not fully develop until the mid- to later-twenties. This is critical information to understand for anyone teaching in post-secondary education. Our college and career readiness instructors need to be prepared for encountering adolescents with behaviors driven by underdeveloped brains. These adolescent brains continue to be wired for novelty, and are at a disadvantage for adequate emotional regulation and impulse control. During adolescence, there is an increase in the activity of the neural circuits using dopamine, a neurotransmitter central in creating our drive for reward.[5]

Starting in early adolescence and peaking midway through, this enhanced dopamine release causes adolescents to seek thrilling experiences and exhilarating sensations. Research even suggests that the baseline level of dopamine in these years is lower—but its release in response to stimulation is higher—which can explain why teens may report a feeling of being "bored" unless they are engaging in stimulating and novel activities.[6]

This enhanced natural dopamine release can give adolescents a powerful sense of being alive when they are engaged in life. It can also lead them to focus solely on the positive rewards they are sure are in store for them, while failing to notice or give value to the potential risks and downsides. During these developmental years, the consistent use of alcohol and drugs can delay prefrontal cortex development. The brain responds to its environment and the developing prefrontal lobes where the executive skills of problem solving, sustained attention, and emotional regulation may be compromised. Post secondary educators need to also pay close attention to these developing years and what is occurring in the brain and how this development affects learning and behaviors.

Social acceptance and social engagement are priorities during this time of development. There is an emotional intensity during these adolescent years that eludes adults. We do not experience this intensity of emotions when encountering experiences and new relationships. Intense emotions rule the days, and the drama of what adults perceive as ordinary is a part of the adolescent pulse. Dr. Dan Seigel identifies the fourth characteristic of adolescent development as creative exploration. He defines this developing thinking as "out of the box," with a questioning mindset that constantly challenges the status quo in an adolescent's life.[7]

I have recently learned just how very significant it is for higher education instructors and professors to understand the complexity of student development upon entering college level courses and classes. Their vulnerability, experiences, and habits, carried through the earlier years in secondary school, do not suddenly disappear over the summer following the senior year. As a mom and an educator, I view brain development as an opportunity as well as a risk. I am becoming aware at home, first hand, of these paradoxes and possibilities in the fragile years of an adolescents' search for meaning, purpose, and autonomy.

Children and adolescents experiencing social pain are hurting from the inside out. They align the world around them with their inner thoughts and feelings, defining personal logic and personhood. Social pain guides how our young people view their world. As adults, our perceptions guide how we view the world too, but our perceptions have been practiced with more reflection and refinement. The truth is, we never stop learning or discovering who we are and what is meaningful to each of us. Although we think we are living consciously, most of us live our daily lives from a subconscious perspective. Children and adolescents who struggle emotionally with feelings of low self-worth and self-efficacy are, oftentimes, replaying old worn-out recordings and scripts from those early years of "how" he or she subconsciously integrated the beliefs and values inside his or her world. As Dr. Nick Long has stated, "What young people believe about themselves is more important in examining their behavior than any facts about them."[8]

What is becoming exceedingly clearer to me with each teaching experience is the importance of attending to the social and emotional brain states of our students as well as their cognitive lives. Yes, I will teach the content based upon the rigorous academic standards promoting high level cognitive processes aligning to content mastery at the fifth, seventh grade, undergraduate, and graduate levels, but there is something greater inside this instruction that creates and possibly drives a growth mindset.[9] Actually children do not learn much from people they do not like.

Over the past few years, I have exercised a new muscle, in the midst of challenging and disagreeable moments and experiences. This new muscle is a perspective muscle. A rapidly growing body of scientific research, conducted by investigators such as Barbara Fredrickson at the University of Michigan, has supported the Dalai Lama's views in finding a strong relationship and correlation between this "broader perspective" and positive emotions. Studies have found that people experiencing positive emotions naturally tend to see things from a broader perspective— they see "the big picture."[10] Conversely, deliberately adopting a broader perspective has been found to increase positive emotions while reducing negative ones. Both positive emotions and a broadened perspective contribute to greater resilience, the capacity and ability to rebound from adversity and individually perceived traumatic experiences.

Much like conditioning an isolated muscle or muscle group in our body, reappraising a thought or a belief is becoming a well-known method of cultivating this broader emotional and cognitive perspective. This is a practice. It asks us, and our students, to deliberately look at problems in new ways, actively discovering some buried positive meaning, higher purpose, or potential benefit related to adversity—either in the short-term or long-term solution. What can we ask ourselves? Can I learn anything from the situation? Can it help me grow in some way and make me stronger? Can it potentially lead to new opportunities, new relationships, or help strengthen old relationships? What are my next two steps? Who or what are my resources? Looking forward, what is one aspect of this problem I can change?

When we begin to understand what happens in the circuitry of our brains as we rethink, reassess, and reframe an old thought, an ineffective thought pattern, or a repetitive unproductive experience, we begin to "feel" that we can influence our circumstances. This, in itself, provides us with a fresh mindset that quietly says, "Maybe I can do this." Questions carry the propensity for awakening the sleeping giant in our subconscious minds that I have named "Attachment."

Simply stated, when we have attached an outcome to an upcoming event, experience, or relationship, we set ourselves up to be continually and consistently disappointed. Our singular ideas, expectations, and solutions, of how a situation should evolve, can prohibit the openness and objectivity needed to understand behaviors and communication at a deeper level.

So what can we do? I believe we can begin to pay attention to the emotional and social regimen of ourselves and our students. The emotional care inside our classrooms has the propensity to create and renew a sense of purpose, feelings of success, and a willingness to persevere from many of our students when adversity strikes. Many of our parents and students walk into our classrooms "carrying in" ambient developmental trauma that has unintentionally and subconsciously become hard-wired in the brain. Trauma has many faces. It can affect all realms inside an individual's life. Trauma's impact on development is profound. There are many sources of trauma: divorce, neglect, homelessness, food instability, and other childhood abuses. Other traumatic events include difficulty sleeping, bullying, and any sudden change in the environment that is perceived as threatening. When children or adolescents live in, or are subjected to, toxic environments for a significant amount of time, this experience can create feelings of shame, causing whole parts of their brains to barely develop. They become adults who are unable to feel a sense of self or pleasure. The world is perceived as a dangerous place, and their brains become locked in a self-protective mode, replaying fear and danger most of the time. Academics will never matter until those emotional states and connections are considered and addressed.

To reframe a scenario, experience, or behavior, we will have more success when we replace a worn-out thought, behavior, or feeling with a novel alternative. It becomes so important in our classrooms to revisit guidelines, rituals, and procedures—often, especially when we feel a stagnant cycle occurring with diminished emotional connections and an inert, apathetic environment. In a living system, the continual exchange of energy, coupled with the hot, messy development of all individuals, calls us to replace the behaviors and circumstances that are no longer serving each of us.

**Survey Results: What does your teacher say to you that feels encouraging or motivating?**

For the past two years, I have surveyed the students and teachers with these two questions in mind. "What does your teacher say to you that feels encouraging or motivating? (What do you think students want to hear from you for encouragement and motivation?) What do you want to hear from a teacher about your performance in school? From a variety of educators (including under-graduates), and students in three large school districts, four elementary and middle schools, the answers to these questions have affirmed how very significant social accept-ance and feeling "felt" are inside of schools.

1. **Believe in Me.** "I believe in you. You are going to be successful someday. You're going to make it! There is nothing holding you back!

To believe in another, is to see what cannot be seen just yet! It takes a focus on all that is going well and right even though there will be conflicts, bad moods, ornery behaviors, and consequences for poor choices. We notice it all—new shoes, hairstyles, kind gestures, (though they may be scattered and few)—and we build upon even the most challenging of performances that could turn on a dime (with a perspective shift) to a *strength*. We are detec-tives, looking for the missing pieces that we know exist, but have been momentarily buried. We create experiences, "forced successes," that give the student an opportunity to feel capable! We can give more choices. We can leave affirming notes and share our personal challenges that caused us to doubt ourselves at an earlier time in our own lives. "I believe in you! Let's make a plan together for just tomorrow. Let's choose two accomplishments you want to see through and design a way for that to happen!"

2. **Help Me Find My Purpose**. "You have a purpose Matt. I see it, and I feel it! Let's have fun and discover what it is. A purpose might change, and that is a good thing, but it's there!" How do we help a student find his or her purpose? We begin with an affirmation, "You have a purpose!" We listen. We listen for interests and signs. We respect the off days and the off hours, and we try again! We share stories of others who lost a bit of hope and purpose, but tried again and again! J.K. Rowling, Bill Gates, Michael Jordan, and Walt Disney are just a few well-known individuals who defined purpose through their mistakes and failures. We talk about the gift of failing and how we can choose to respond and learn from those moments of illusory despair. We begin to create a "purpose" for those students at school and in our classrooms. We make a plan— a plan to invite the student to *serve another*. Maybe he or she tutors a younger student or helps to plan a surprise meal for the custodians and the cafeteria staff. Maybe she targets another student who is struggling, becoming a secret inspirer for a week. Maybe we connect the class to a retirement home and Skype with another generation who has lived through these tumultuous years yet would love the companionship and communication from middle and high school students. Field trips are fewer today, and this allows us to invite community members with their own purposes and gifts to be guests in our classrooms, igniting and sharing the work they are doing with homeless populations, incarcerated youth, and other service organizations that thrive on volunteerism.

3. **Question Me.** Ask me how I am. Ask me what I need. Ask me my thoughts and feelings. Ask me what my opinions are, even if my response is ridiculous because I don't want to stand out in front of my peers! Ask me in private—always in private. Ask me to teach you! Ask me to teach you anything about my world, my culture, music I love, my beliefs and my story. I may not say a word, and it may take the entire school year for me to respond to your questions, but I hear you. I hear your interest, your compassionate concern for what I like, what I need, and what plans I would like to create.

When we serve another, our own neurobiological and emotional circuitry changes, shifting into the prefrontal lobes and away from the survival stress response When we reach out and connect with others, our perspectives broaden, increasing positive emotion, while enhancing our own feelings of purpose and well-being.

*Every child and adolescent needs at least one adult who is irrationally crazy about him or her.*
URIE BRONFENBRENNER

### Parents as Partners / The Key to Connection

The old adage of a triangular model where educators, students, and parents are working alongside one another sounds terrific, typed up on this word document, but how do we actualize this partnership, breathing life into the equity and respect we desire from one another? From years of sitting on both sides of the conference table, I feel parent-educator collaboration and effectiveness occurs when there is a mutual openness for change. But, the only aspect of this collaborative process that is in our control is our own shift or change in perspective. When we gather into groups of living systems, we bring in our values, beliefs, and histories because the brain is not only a social organ but an historical organ. We carry in ideas and feelings that, in the moment, are the best we have. As teachers and administrators, we sometimes project ourselves onto our parents, attaching biases and stereotypes that simply are not very accurate. We hold tightly to our values and forget that sometimes these middle class values are not aligned to the students and families we serve.

Dr. Nick Long, founder of the Life Space Crisis Intervention Institute, has identified several middle class values, of which we must be very aware and careful not to project onto our families and students. These values are not right or wrong and really exist along a continuum. Some of the more common middle class values include our ideas about cleanliness and neatness. From the time we were babies, to be clean and neat were virtues. A "neat" person is appealing and messiness is the enemy. Another common middle class value is to be hard-working. A person who enjoys hard work, never gives up, and perseveres. Lazy people have no standards and are passive and idle. Emotional control is another value of the middle class. You are safe to be with, self-directed, mature, and dependable. Emotionally explosive people are dangerous and unpredictable. Often middle class values are highly prized and are the invisible cultural water within our schools and educational institutions. For example, do you remember how important it was to be "on time" in school? Students actually get punished for being a few minutes late in our schools and very few adults within that culture would even question that value. These values become a problem when we hold them up as virtues that all people are to be judged by. We need to become very mindful of the values that we hold up as virtues in our schools. Many times, we may be pre-judging our students and their families when we suggest that these often unstated values must be upheld or demon-strated by all.[11]

There is not a parent on this planet who awakens in the morning desiring negative experiences and hardships for their children. And yet, when students walk in late, do not complete their homework assignments, lose text-books, or behave inappropriately, we often want to place blame on the parents or families. We sometimes are very quick to judge and blame others for things that frustrate us. Below is a stereotype reported in Dr. Paul Gorski's *Reaching Students in Poverty*:

The most popular measure of parental attitudes about education, particularly among teachers, is "family involve-ment" (Jeynes 2011). This stands to reason, as research consistently confirms a correlation between family involve-ment and school achievement (Lee and Bowen 2006; Oyserman, Brickman, and Rhodes 2007). However, too often, our notions of family involvement are limited in scope, focused only on in-school involvement—the kind of involvement that requires parents and guardians to visit their children's schools or classrooms. While it is true that low-income parents and guardians are less likely to participate in this brand of "involvement" (National Center for Educational Statistics 2005), they engage in home-based involvement strategies, such as encouraging children to read and limiting television watching, more frequently than their wealthier counterparts (Lee and Bowen 2006).[12]

Engagement with parents is critical and this process begins to occur when we drop our personal biases and assumptions, recognizing that we each want the best for the child or adolescent. When educators and parents feel understood and supported, children and adolescents reap the ongoing benefits of a collective assemblage who are aware and are adjusting and listening to the needs of one another. This doesn't always occur because even as adults, we mimic the emotions of one another and are triggered to move swiftly into our fight or flight response when we feel our values and beliefs have been challenged. Below are a few sparks that may ignite collaboration and a more empathetic environment from all those sitting beside our students.

## SPARKS

1. **Plan VIP Parent Nights**—for parents to meet, eat, and share their expertise in any area. Celebrate parents! Even if they do not attend, call them or write to them, and tell them how grateful you are that they have shared their child with you. Ask parents to bring in their expertise: hair styling, office work, or any part of the vocation or profession in which they are involved.

2. **Positive Notes**—at least once a week. Even if there have been discipline issues, it is our responsibility to share one or two positive behaviors from the day or week. Michael and I term these "positive referral sheets," which track movement and progress, not the end goal. This can be a checklist or a brief statement of what you appreciated this week from this student.

3. **Homework**—look beneath the reasons students are not completing or turning in homework on time, or at all. Are they held accountable at home? What happens

when students do not turn in homework? Is the homework realistic, and is it a review of what the student knows or has learned? Are we focusing on the concept to be learned and not the number of problems or length of assignments? A good rule of thumb is to create assignments that equate to five minutes of homework per grade level. For example, first grade would have a review of material for five minutes with second grade at ten minutes. We can model homework in the classroom in a manner that shows we can really have fun with this! We often assume our students know "how" to do homework. In class, we can create a stage where we pretend this is our bedroom or kitchen at home. In this space, we set up a working homework station and actually go through all the steps for a successful twenty minutes of reviewing or creating. Grab a snack, lay out all materials, pull out directions, and make sure the environment is distraction free. Students will love to see you play act and pretend while teaching the behaviors you desire to see with regard to homework.

We need to be creative and resourceful with regard to grading homework and aware of the environments students are entering when they leave school. Brainstorm with students other times, environments, and ways they can check for understanding and learn the content in deeper ways. When students are a part of the plan, they are much more likely to put forth effort and motivation. We need to remember that homework is practice. Practice needs to be reinforced with skills the students know well. Nothing good comes from poor practice and errors are only reinforced when students work independently with minimally learned subject matter.

# Self-Assessments

The following self-assessment survey, created for students and educators, provides questions that address short- and long-term goals. In doing so, it provides a framework for metacognition (thinking about our thoughts) and helps us each to clarify, reflect on, and prioritize our feelings, actions, and behaviors. It allows us to begin feeling a sense of autonomy throughout our learning processes.

EDUTOPIA CHART

http://www.edutopia.org/pdfs/blogs/edutopia-desautels-SEL-rubric.pdf

I designed this rubric for educators to share with students so that daily standards, subject matter, and behaviors presented in the classroom and schools can reflect the integration of significant and smaller incremental goals. This is where the rubber meets the road because when any of us emotionally experiences the connections to what we do and say, either in alignment with our desires and plans or completely off the intended track, we can become intrinsically motivated to pursue those short-term goals. And we know that, in the process, we not only begin to *feel* better, but we also begin to see and reap the benefits of our efforts. These come through making mistakes, confronting challenges, and seeing through a lens that is broader than the classroom walls. They become helpful perspectives and resources in self-perseverance, creative visualizations, and self-awareness.

## Big Goals

1. Completed a project successfully
2. Obtained a summer job
3. Volunteered as peer tutor or advocate
4. Presented in a class or organization
5. Submitted a manuscript (short story, poem, began writing a book, etc.)
6. Volunteered at a non-profit organization
7. Improved grades in school
8. Joined other organization or clubs

## Daily Goals

1. Completed work
2. Dialogued about frustrations
3. Stayed focused on assignments
4. Showed respect and compassion for others
5. Regrouped and continued on with work after a frustrating time
6. Helped a teacher or student
7. Contributed some ideas and suggestions to a conversation
8. Used positive self-talk when describing a need or desire
9. Self-reflected how my daily work and interactions affect my big goals
10. Shared big goals with parents, administrators, and community members
11. Created a personal statement, visual, and/or tool for encouragement when working on big goals

For more chart, goals, and self-assessment information: http://www.edutopia.org/blog/self-assessment-inspires-learning-lori-desautels.[13]

# CHAPTER 5

# The Story of Active Hope

### THRIVE

T—Trust
H—Hope
R—Respect
I—Imagine/ Innovate
V—Validate
E—Empathy

### MICHAEL & LORI

**W**E SEE STUDENTS survive every day. As educators and parents, we often feel that *we* barely survive each day. We survive a class, a test, a conflict, a relationship, and a perceived challenge; yet, surviving is very different than thriving. Many of the students that we see every day bring a degree of stress with them into our classrooms. Thankfully many of them also have supports in their lives that allow them to manage this stress in a productive manner. Our most difficult students however are not as lucky. They live in a state of chronic toxic stress. Chronic toxic stress changes the brain. This level of stress literally places their brains in survival mode. If the brain is in a survival response, its creative, resourceful, and imaginative higher-level thought processes are compromised because of emotions and thoughts that feel unsafe and threatening. When we feel guilt, shame, anger, sadness, or any negative emotion, over an extended period of time, our brains begin to create neural pathways that ignite habits of feelings in response to the thoughts that call forth these feelings and emotions. Neural traits become brain states. These neural pathways become difficult to change. We settle. We create a victim stance. We react rather than respond, and although our biology is also predisposed to survival instincts, paradoxically we have the capacity and ability to be mindfully present with one another. In healthy environments that nurture us, our species is neurobiologically wired to thrive. When human beings have their developmental needs met, we unfold naturally, and that unfolding guides us in discovering our natural gifts and to thrive.

*If kids come to us from strong, healthy, functioning families,*
*it makes our job easier. If they do not come to us*
*from strong, healthy, functioning families,*
*it makes our job more important.*
BARBARA COLOROSE

When we are living in environments of toxic stress our brains literally downshift to a survival mode. We literally are immersed in a fight, flight, freeze response mode. Under these conditions, left without supports, we learn to survive rather than thrive. These are the children and youth that enter our schools and need more from us.

Often they are our most difficult students. How do we begin to work successfully with these children and youth? The teaching sparks in this chapter are embedded throughout the THRIVE acronym. You will discover many sparks for you and your students as we delve into trust, hope, respect, imagination, and empathy.

## 1. "T" for Trust

*Trust between a child and adult is essential, the foundation on which all other principles rest, the glue that holds teaching and learning together . . .*
NICHOLAS HOBBS

Trust is the foundation of how we relate to people in this world. If the process of trust is not established, as so many researchers have reported and validated, then we have challenging times with students (and adults) who feel and act disconnected and detached in ways that grow opposition, aggression, shame, hurt, and hopelessness.

Trust begins with a child or adolescent "knowing" a teacher is present. Students who have experienced trauma, neglect, and circumstances that have low levels of trust and connections throughout their lives, are literally swimming in pain. The majority of your most difficult students have a developmental history filled with negative experiences. If we simply look at their school history, it is filled with discipline referrals, unsuccessful punitive interventions, and sustained failure. If we examine their life experiences outside of school, we will find a pattern of prolonged adult rejection, neglect, and often abuse. It is critical for educators working with these young people to know that their history has conditioned them to see any new staff relationship as toxic and potentially hostile. Creating positive connections with students who are swimming in pain, and building trust with these young people, is an endurance event! They will initially and sometimes literally "bite the hand that attempts to feed them." Trust must be built slowly over time. How can we begin to successfully "reclaim" these young people?

First they will need to know that "we are not going away." We are present for them no matter their behaviors, outward intentions, or hurtful words. The resiliency research is clear and very hopeful to anyone working with troubled children and youth. One person can make a positive impact and turn lives around. Bonnie Benard (2007), a leader in the field of resiliency, calls these educators, turnaround teachers,[1] as we have previously stated.

Research reports that the single most central factor in building relationships and trust is an act of caring compassion. For many children and adolescents who have spent a lifetime in adverse environments, their stress response systems are in a chronic level of allostasis. This means they are hyper vigilant and reactive in all areas of their life. They are so accustomed to fighting, freezing, or fleeing, their ability to think through a learning problem and to emotionally soothe and redirect are shut down and off. It is critical to remember that our most troubled students are *led by their feelings*. They feel and react. During these times, often untrained and well-meaning educators can easily get caught in escalating conflict cycles that end up damaging the connections we need to forge with these students. We, too, get caught up in fight/flight/freeze responses because emotions are highly contagious.

To connect with our most difficult youth we must learn the skills necessary to react differently. Recently researchers have been studying another less common reaction to stress called "tend and befriend."[2] They propose that females often respond to stress in a different manner. Tending involves nurturing activities designed to protect the young, while befriending is the creation of social networks that reduce stress and provide supports for all people in the environment. During times of escalating stress with young people, the concept of tending and befriending rather than our fight/flight/freeze responses can be learned. We can literally choose not to fight with young people.

During these times of high stress it becomes critical for staff to provide "emotional first aid"[3] for these students. If we can demonstrate that we can be with students at their "worst," and assist them in calming down and problem solving, we begin to build trust. Rather than becoming caught up in an escalating conflict that damages the relationship, we can begin to learn the skills that will allow us to drain off their hostility and frustration, affirm their feelings, separate those feelings from their behaviors, and begin to teach them to problem solve. These all fall into the concept of "tending behaviors." We must recognize that punishment is toxic to young people who have suffered from neglect, rejection, and abuse. *The central problem for educators working with children and youth that demonstrate "pain-based behaviors" is our ability to handle their primary pain without inflicting secondary pain-filled experiences in an attempt to teach them how to behave.* We can begin to do this by shifting how we handle problem behaviors and by changing our view and seeing these difficult behaviors as opportunities to teach young people how to problem solve and manage conflicts. We teach rather than punish. We can literally tend to their needs and build their skills rather than cause more pain.

We find the following words from a past president of the National Association of State Directors of Special Education a helpful reminder of how we can begin to make this critical shift:

> If a child does not know how to read, we teach.
> If a child does not know how to swim, we teach.
> If a child does not know how to multiply, we teach.
> If a child does not know how to drive, we teach.
> If a child does not know how to behave, we....[4]

We also know that affirmation, attention, and availability help to foster healthy relationships with others. These three "A"s also assist in developing the most significant relationship in all our lives that we sometimes neglect. This relationship is the one we have with ourselves. As we move through life experiences, we need to remember to listen to our own minds and hearts—affirming and giving attention to our purpose while being available to ourselves for rest and self-reflection as we create a stream of well-being, no matter the view on the outside. We can learn to create and carry our own "mind" weather.

How do we sit beside our students helping them to find the deeper meaning and purpose inside themselves? It is challenging during the adolescent years, as peers become the key players. How can we begin to develop emotional fitness in the minds of our students when their life experiences have been filled, and are filled, with significant and repetitive adversity?

First we begin to *be present*. We notice everything and learn as much as we can about our students! We comment on their new shoes, hairstyles, their smiles, and just simply notice who they are and let them know that we are glad to see them. We learn that we must pick and choose our battles and that not all behaviors we dislike or disagree with will go away. We learn to affirm those behaviors and conversations that serve them well, building on their capacities to learn, to relate, and to connect with someone who understands and shares their challenges.

To be attentive and affirmative is to begin teaching the student rather than the curriculum. Yes it is important to teach content; however, it is critical that we always recognize that our students are more important than our subjects and standards. We must demonstrate that we care. At the core of helping and healing is the act of caring. It is rarely spoken about or thoroughly presented in teacher preparation programs; yet, it is a critical component of effective teaching. Students that feel known and cared about will be much more motivated to learn, and as Nel Nodding has said:

*"At a time when the traditional structures of caring have deteriorated, schools must become places where teachers and students live together, talk with each other, take delight in each other's company . . . it is obvious that children will work harder and do things for people they like and trust."*[5]

It is important to add that caring is not enough. Teachers must also develop the skill of creating structure and order without the use of coercion. Chaos is viewed by students as unsafe and also uncaring. We structure our environments to provide our students with a sense of safety and predictability, and we structure our instruction to provide all students with a felt sense of success.

We know many of our students are shutting off academically because they are not feeling successful. Every single child or adolescent will always choose to be perceived as "bad" rather than dumb or stupid! When we understand this unspoken truth, we begin to build and create short mini-lessons where we know students will be successful. This is a process and a starting place. As my friend and educator Michael McKnight explains, "We can force success." We oftentimes teach way beyond a student's skill set. Relearning developmental psychologist Lev Vygotsky's "Zone of Proximal Development"[6] is a great place for us to start. We must literally create islands of competency for young people who have experienced nothing but failure since they entered school. To begin developing layers of trust, we must meet the student where he or she is, developing a plan of action that is saturated with a sense of belonging and capability.

We can also begin to teach and model how building upon our own passions, strengths, and challenges draws the people, experiences, and life events that support and cultivate our own minds and hearts. How do we begin to support students in trusting himself/ herself and others? We model and teach what we want to see more of from our students. Authentic emotions, thoughts, action steps, and ideas that we share initiate this process. We are wired to mimic one another. Mirror neurons in our brains support the idea of modeling for our students.[7] Modeling the behaviors we would like to see from our students, as we work with them to replace the behaviors that are less than positive, will quiet their hot reactions, leading them down a more positive path. Feelings of success breed more success.

A simple place to start our modeling is with a commitment to ourselves that we will treat all students with a high degree of dignity and respect regardless of how they are currently treating us. This will require us to model "self-discipline," which is the ability to regulate our own emotions, a skill many of our most troubled children and youth desperately need to learn.

Learning Logs are another wonderful resource for implementing mutual trust in our classrooms. When we record our own observations, ideas, and what we have learned from our students, we are indirectly encouraging them to assess, self-reflect, and discover a novel idea, connection, or behavior. In this Learning Log, we will record noticed behaviors as well as academic ideas. Time will be designated a few minutes a day, to record and consolidate the academic learning and dispositions observed inside of our classrooms. We will also share our perspectives, creating an atmosphere that feels trusting and non-threatening.

We are learning that all we ask from our students we must be ready to attempt ourselves. If I have given students an assignment, a directive, or a consequence, it is my responsibility to meet the students in the middle. Trust is built through attention, availability, and affirmation. We begin to share our mistakes. We apologize when we have become angry in a way that is non-productive. We talk aloud about the choices we see in a particular situation, weighing our options, as we move closer to solutions or decisions. We listen hard with the intent to learn and understand. When a rule is broken, we share our concern and, of course, the consequence, but we are clear that behaviors are actions, and they do not define our sacred personhood. More importantly, we take the time to not just deliver consequences from a pre-existing list of "dos and don'ts," but begin to problem solve with students, gaining a commitment to do things differently the next time.

We need to be aware of the timing of a consequence, knowing that conflict cycles can escalate or diminish based on our delivery, tone, and authenticity. It is very important that both the adult and the student are purposefully acting from the problem solving part of their brains, not merely reacting to situations or peer/teacher stimuli. It is my honor and responsibility to teach a desirable skill or behavior that I'm not currently experiencing in the classroom from a student. As a twenty-first century educator, in the story of *now*, I have several opportunities each day to share, discuss, and provide opportunities to model a new way of being with one's learning or inside a struggling relationship.

Building trust requires robust conversations at a neutral time, when the brain states of both teacher and student are primed for listening and learning. When we have those discussions, we make sure to share similar personal experiences and the choices we made that did or did not serve us well. If we cannot come up with a poor choice we've made in the past, then we listen deeply, knowing we will come away from this conversation with knowledge that we didn't have before an incident occurred. We share a presence with our students so that they know we're one hundred percent available. In building trust, we also let go of the problem and return to a place where we both begin again. To actually let go of a student's poor choice is to model with our verbal and nonverbal communication, "I can see potential. I see what you are unable to see at this time! We will give this another go . . . "

A very easy way to send this message is to post what Grace Pilon calls *truth signs*.[8] Truth signs are not typical signs you see in a classroom. They simply remind the class of important truths about living and learning. Here are a few examples, but feel free to create your own.

· It's OK to make mistakes. That's the way we learn.

- If it happened it happened. Let's learn, problem solve, and move on.
- Life is not always easy. It can call us to stretch and grow.
- Know what your best effort is and strive to do it every day.

What might be some of the truth signs you would highlight in your classroom?

Rarely do we discuss hope as part of our role as educators, but educators can be inspirers of hope. Hope is defined as a feeling or expectation and desire for a certain thing to happen.

## 2. "H" for Hope

Hope can have an activating effect on us and our students. We must provide students with a reason to come to school every day! When we model hope for our students, we are actually sharing our heartaches, celebrations, and small steps with every emotion that occurred in reaching our goals. Hope begins with questions. When we question our goals, plans, and intentions, we help develop a sense of active hope. Activating hope is about becoming lively participants in bringing about what we hope for. This is the antidote to despair and to hopelessness that lies beneath much of the behavior we see from our most troubled children.

What do you hope for today? What do you hope for this week? How do you get there? What will it take to make this desire a reality? Is the hope you have for this relationship, experience, or event something you can work towards? Is your "hope" something you can control? If the hope lies outside our control, then we must model for our students what is within our power and control. *We must help one another to understand that hope is the roadmap in a destination of perspective.* If I perceive something as good, bad, right, or wrong, then it is! My thoughts have labeled an experience based on only my views and outlook. If I hope my parents get back together, then the hope I hold is outside of my control. If I hope I pass my test on Thursday, then I have the tools, time, and mindset to fulfill my desires. If I hope that my boyfriend does not break up with me, then once again, I am relying on other people, thoughts, and experiences that are out of my control. I can perceive or treat a break-up as a positive or negative happening based on my outlook.

As a teacher, I cannot only model how hope plays out in my own life, but I can give my students hope by noticing all that is going right and well. I can choose to focus on the most mundane and obvious task or action, knowing it is an improvement and movement from an hour ago, the morning, yesterday, or week before.

Each day we can create a dialogue of "hindsight moments." When we share our choices and disappointments based on a past experience, highlighting the reasons, lessons learned, and experiences we would have never encountered, we are sharing the gift of hope.

For younger students, hope begins when we assist our children in self-assessing their work, actions, and behaviors. Questions such as: What do you think? How do you feel this turned out? Let's make a plan! What are the two most important things we can do to make this happen? How is your plan working out? What could you do differently? Where could we go for help?

When we begin to sit beside our students encouraging

them to self-assess behaviors and schoolwork, we are empowering them with their own aptitudes and voices. When mistakes are seen as tools for learning, we begin to feel safe and to trust the process of our thoughts and work, rather than always looking at the end results and for others' judgments and evaluations.

> *Hoping is often confused with wishing. But hope is grounded in realism, not in wishful thinking.*
>
> THOMAS J. SERGIOVANI,
> IN *STRENGTHENING THE HEARTBEAT*

Menninger, Mayman, and Pruyser write about realistic hope, which they define as the attempt to understand the concrete conditions of reality, to see one's own role in it realistically, and to engage in such efforts of thoughtful action as might be expected to bring about the hoped-for change. The activating effect of hope makes the difference. Some education communities engage in wishful thinking but take no deliberate action to make their wishes come true. Hopeful education communities, in contrast, take action to turn their hopes into reality.[9]

We must move our educational community toward taking hopeful actions.

### 3. "R" for Respect

Respect is difficult to define and measure. Because we are a living organic system, our definitions, interpretations, feelings, and history matter greatly as we try and implement an element of respect in our classrooms. We can sit in meetings and community circles all day long discussing how respect looks in a classroom, but it may not feel personal or meaningful.

Respect begins when we walk our students' walk. What I ask of my students, I too must be willing to invest the effort to accomplish. When respect is demonstrated in any environment there is a beneficial tone, a facial expression, and a posture that listens to learn. This type of deep respectful listening communicates our message to students that we are always willing to separate the behavior of the individual from the individual. It is a process of creating a place and space that understands timing, and there is also an understanding that each person is doing his/her best in the moment.

As educators, are we inwardly prepared to adjust our mindsets, open our beliefs, and risk a little of our pride to see through a different lens? Are we willing to listen and to be changed by what it is we hear?

When educators and parents can design, verbalize, and openly share our own *learning and coping strategies*, we are modeling transparency, creativity, and tangible respect to our children and adolescents. What is your learning strategy? How do you approach new material? How do you memorize? How do you retrieve information? What do you say to yourself? What or who are your resources? How do you learn new information? How do you make connections between what you already know and what is being taught? As I stand before fifth- and seventh-grade students, I begin to share, "For me, I need to read out loud while writing key words down in my notebook or textbook! I also use lots of colors to help address the most important parts I need to memorize." Then the sharing begins. One student at a time begins to describe how he or she approaches new material and how they think and feel about it. We decide as a class that instead of a periodic chart, with listed elements, we will create a periodic table with learning strategies. We decide upon which wall to place this large colorful chart and then we discuss how seeing the different learning strategies will help us to choose one that we might have never considered.

What are your coping strategies when experiences in life get you down? How do you cope with emotional and social adversities and challenges in your life? How do you repair, reappraise, and put back together difficult times and experiences? How do you begin again? Do you blame? Is your heart an active part of this process? Do you feel frozen with worry and fear, and if so, how do you move out of these feelings?

We feel it is so helpful to share and model a scenario with our students. For me, I give myself a good "talking to" in private. Here is what it may sound like. "Lori, take a deep breath or two and know that this problem has a solution somewhere in your brain. Let's just list all the reasons this might have happened and what you can begin to do with these options!" The students laugh a little and talk amongst themselves for a few minutes. We then slowly begin to share our coping strategies as a class! Some of the strategies discussed are: taking a walk, spending some time alone, talking the problem out with others, eating some ice cream or Wheat Thins, and moving away from the challenge for a little while. This list begins to grow, and purposefully we have created another colorful wall of emotional coping strategies in a periodic table format. The students understand that this colorful array of strategies allows them to choose a strategy that they might never have thought of in a heightened emotional moment.

Do you have a plan of action for your academic and emotionally challenging times? These types of preventative action plans that we are defining as learning and coping strategies are vital if we desire to address the "whole" student. When I share my learning and coping strategies with students, I am not only modeling and teaching behaviors I want to see in my classroom, but I am indirectly saying to each individual, "You have the potential, now how do you accomplish this?"

How could we use and implement these strategies inside our assessments, instruction, and in our classroom cultures? We need to develop these learning and coping strategy plans across all grade levels. Our habits of learning, as well as our habits of emotionally coping, begin to define how we walk through relationships, events, and life.

## 4. "I" for Imagination and Innovation

Imagination is the oxygen of life! It is our natural human birthright and we are all born with this potential to design, play, make meaning, and think in novel ways. As adults we oftentimes revert back to what feels safe and familiar, unintentionally welcoming the habit-mind that has subconsciously formed alongside routines that have replaced spontaneity. Imagination is critical for academic success, and it actually rests at the foundation of our learning and motivation.

Albert Einstein conducted "thought experiments" that enabled him to make cognitive leaps that other scientists of his time could not. It wasn't about his determination or brainpower. The difference, according to biographer Walter Issacson, was imagination. Einstein knew he needed to visualize his ideas in novel ways. It is within imaginative and visual thinking that the power of questions becomes so significant to learning. When we ask questions, the brain processes these much longer than statements because statements motivate people to agree or disagree. Questions present a mind puzzle and roadmap. Below are some of the questions Issacson suggests relating to goals, decisions, conflicts, and challenges.[10]

What does success look like in this situation?

If resources were not constrained, what could be possible here?

What are the most pressing issues or challenges you face?

If we were to create the perfect solution for you, what would that look like?

Why is this need important to you?

What are your criteria for making this decision? Why?

What options did you consider and reject?

What did we learn from this situation?

What would we do differently in the future?

How and where else can we apply this learning for greater success?

What are your goals in this situation?

What are some constraints you're facing and what would be possible if they were removed?

How can I support you in that?

Why is this goal really important to me? What is already working well?

What have I done to create that success?

What special talents or strengths do I have that can help me achieve my goals?

What are strengths I have that can be leveraged at work?

What brings me joy in the work that I do?

How can my strengths, taken to an extreme, become derailers for me?

Creating thought experiments could be an activity we implement with our students once a week. In this designated time, we lead our students as we play with a personal project we are working through and can share with our students. These projects could be ongoing or they could be different each day. People are hard-wired and attracted to both rituals and novelty. On these allocated days or parts of the day, teachers could decorate the room as a science or think tank lab. The entrance to our classrooms could invite innovation, creativity, and imagination through posters, wall or desk signage, and greeters. Outside guests or community experts in different areas could assist in these thought experiment days by sharing their challenges and how they envisioned, took incremental steps, and planned through their ideas.

### 5. and 6. "V" for Validate and "E" for Empathize

Validation and empathy are the hand and glove to a student's feeling of purpose, autonomy, and mastery. Validation is a research-based strategy that promotes an extremely positive emotion of "feeling felt." When one feels that another truly understands and knows how an event and/ or relationship has been experienced, we are inclined to trust and share more information with that individual. Below are some examples of validating the pain-based words that are often expressed in reactive, hot, messy moments, when feelings of pain and shame have exploded into emotions of hurt and hopelessness. It is during these times that we can unintentionally enter into a conflict cycle, personalizing the overt language.

Every day we observe all of these developing minds and hearts of our students, trying to find their place, purpose, and way in the world. My question is: How would relationships and conversations change if we could decode and understand the feelings beneath the inappropriate, disrespectful, and hurtful behaviors? I believe we would choose different responses and communication strategies. Below are some recent examples of student responses we have heard over the past several months in moments when students have felt a sense of hopelessness, shame, and intense anger.

The student response is first. The possible deeper meaning, or underlying feelings that our students are trying to convey, is second. (In moments of escalating conflict:)

"Go ahead, I don't care. —————— "

**"Nothing matters right now, and whatever you say to me or do to me will just add to the troubles I am facing and feeling!"**

• • • •

"Whatever! ————————————- "

"We are so far apart on our views, it doesn't matter, because you will never walk my walk."

. . . .

"You think I care? —————"

"What you don't realize is that I am protecting myself and defending all I have . . . myself!"

. . . .

"I wasn't even talking! You didn't get mad at her! ————— "

"Life feels very unfair to me, and no matter what I say, when I say it, or what I do . . . it is always my fault."

. . . .

"Oh My God!! ————— "

"You, again, are so far off from understanding or HEARING me . . . I don't want a relationship with you!" I cannot trust you!"

. . . .

"I'm over it! ————— "

"I need you to give me some space and time. Come back when you are ready to listen to learn . . . instead of listening to respond."

. . . .

"F*** you! —————— "

"I'm so angry, and you cannot possibly understand how I feel!"

. . . .

From our experiences and perspective, these student responses originate from a perception of "lack" and "scarcity," so what they are really stating is, "I am not enough." Feelings of shame create a self-protective and self-destructive cycle; oftentimes, teachers see this pattern more than any other adults! I believe this is why Functional Behavioral Assessments can be so helpful in our classrooms because it causes us, the educators, to look at the antecedents, the behaviors, and consequences of an event or experience. Done well, a Functional Behavioral Assessment will look beneath the surface behavior and begin to address the unmet needs that this student's behavior is trying to communicate.[11]

The most helpful strategy in this type of escalating conflict is really not a strategy, but a way of being in dialogue and checking in with ourselves and our students. In pressure-filled moments when tempers are hot, this is challenging. Our responses are closely observed by our students. If modeling is one of the best practices we can employ, then modeling kindness and a personally detached, yet positive dialogue is key in understanding the underlying needs of so many of our struggling youth.

Questions are processed in the brain long after they have been asked, so the power of providing a question for deepened understanding provides an opportunity for our children and teens to answer in a completely different tone and direction. These responses call for "time" in between a negative reaction and a needed conversation. Sometimes we almost feel frantic to get the consequence into place—NOW! We can provide a consequence, but we can also provide it when there is more felt neutrality between teachers and students.

### Some questions and statements that provoke deepened understanding

1. I know you are so angry! I also feel I could never know what it feels like to be in your shoes. But if you feel like sharing what happened, I can promise you I will listen—and listen closely.

2. It must feel so frustrating to come into this classroom and always feel that you are being picked on, or you are unable to do something successfully! What can I do? What do you need from me to feel even just a little better this morning?

3. Is there anything about you, your life, or experiences that you could share so that I could know more about how we can work this out together? Can you tell me anything else that would be helpful to understand?

4. I am learning every day, just as you are, and honestly, I become frustrated sometimes because I don't have time to get to know everyone better. What more can you share that would help me to understand?

5. Do you think we could create a plan for the two of us? How could we develop some type of communication or agreement where we meet each other half way? (This could be a behavior agreement, homework agreement, etc.)

6. Do you think or feel at some point you might want to share your challenges or frustrations with other students, because chances are your frustrations or upsets are also theirs. I see your strong mind and deep feelings, and these form a perfect equation for being a leader! How could you serve others in our school as you learn more about yourself? Could we make a plan for this over the semester or in the next few weeks?

7. If it is difficult to put into words. Could you explain your feelings or the situation in another way? Art? Music? Poetry? Is there anything from home that you would like to share that would help me to understand more of "who you are"?

*So many people (children and youth) are shut up tight inside themselves like boxes, yet they would open up, unfolding quite wonderfully if only you were interested in them.*

SYLVIA PLATH

Although much of this chapter focuses on troubled children and youth, we want all children that we meet and teach in some capacity to "THRIVE" in our schools! To thrive is to unfold in one's unique way in school environments that focus on the cognitive, emotional, social, physical, and spiritual needs of all students. Using the acronym "THRIVE," we began by defining this as:

**T—Trust.** Trust is built through our ability to empathize with our students and care for them. Building trust is a slow process, and with our most troubled children, an endurance event. Trust is built within environments of a caring presence. We believe that the total school environment needs to be this place for all students.

**H—(Active) Hope.** All children and youth need to have a possible vision of their hoped-for future. In Lisa Delpit's *Other People's Children*, the author describes her experience with hope and "turnaround teachers" this way: "They [teachers] held visions of us that we could not imagine for ourselves. All children need to see new possibilities, and all children need a reason to come to school the next day."[12]

**R—Respect.** Respect must be demonstrated by adults and modeled for children. Children raised in disrespectful ways cannot possibly show respect. Adults, regardless of the child's behaviors, must always show respect and dignity for the child. One of our great challenges is to recognize that the most troubled children and youth will only begin to respond to us when we can demonstrate that we can see them "at their worst" and still provide care, structure, and support in a respectful manner. We must take the initial steps to model respectfulness and dignity to our most difficult children and youth.

**I—Imagination and Innovation.** In some professions there are certainties that act as rules to follow and hold true for the majority of problems or circumstances that may come up. Teaching is not one of those professions! There are very few certainties in our work. Many times we have found ourselves surprised to actually see what has worked in the classroom and what has turned out to be a disaster. Many times what we try as teachers does not work according to our plans. We must consciously recognize that our ability to imagine different ways of teaching a concept, or interacting with a volatile student, is a skill that we can develop over time. Our ability to innovate, to problem solve, and come up with a new idea or plan allows us to face many of the failed efforts that are unavoidable as teachers. We learn and we change and we go on. Our ability to reflect, to own and speak to our mistakes, and then to try again, may be one of the most important lessons we model to our children and youth.

**V—Validation.** What is validation and why is it important? When we validate a student, we are essentially saying, "I see and understand how you are feeling. Your feelings are important to me, and it's okay that you feel that way." Validation provides "psychological air"[13] and allows another the experience of "feeling felt" and understood. We do not need to agree with what the person is feeling, but we do need to acknowledge it. It is about valuing another person's experience and feelings. Validation is the gateway for allowing another his or her experience and self-reflection. Sometimes, to be heard is enough to begin the healing process.

**E—Empathize.** Empathy is our ability to see an event from each individual student's point of view, feeling emotion as if these were our own. It is the key to seeing beneath a student's surface behavior, as we walk inside our students' "private realities." All surface behaviors make sense when we can begin to see through our students' eyes and perspectives. Author Steven Covey explains: "Seek first to understand, and then be understood."[14] Empathy and validation open the door to the conversations we need to have with our children and youth. These conversations can set the trajectory for emotional connections, which leads to children and adolescents who trust.

Yes, there will be hours and days when we simply cannot muster the energy or desire for much beyond surviving, but our ability to return to resiliency and hope can be taught! The growing and brilliant research of neuroplasticity, the brain's ability to change and adapt, is laying the foundations for such strivings and new beginnings.

We believe the concepts reflected in THRIVE are foundational to teaching and learning.

*Children don't care how much you know until*
*they know how much you care.*
JOHN MAXWELL

# CHAPTER 6

# The Story of Well-Being
## *The Way of the Teacher*

### MICHAEL

To TRANSFORM EDUCATION in our country will require much more than what is currently considered best practice in our field. I am currently in my thirty-sixth year as a teacher and still have not mastered the craft of teaching. The current story of becoming a teacher is one filled with rubrics and test scores. It is a story that suggests that to become a highly proficient teacher, all one needs to do is follow a prescriptive rubric and steps that are defined on a state or district template. These are helpful, but they do not embrace the emotional connections and organic communication that builds relationships and, therefore, the craft of teaching. This current prescriptive story suggests that to create master teachers we can use these rubrics, tie them into test scores, and we will be able to definitively identify master teachers.

One of the most recycled rubric frameworks in this story is Charlotte Danielson's framework for teaching.

Many of the current rubrics that districts and states are using to inform teacher practice and evaluation can be traced to Danielson's work. Others include familiar names in education circles, such as Marzano and Strong.

Danielson's framework includes information concerning the following topics: Planning and Preparation, Classroom Environment, Professional Responsibilities, Instruction, and Student Growth. All told, Danielson's 2013 Framework, downloaded from the Internet, is over one hundred pages long and consists of four domains and twenty-two indicators. Each indicator defines one aspect of a domain. We mention all of the rubric components because these indicators and domains are currently implemented to assess and change teaching and learning. They are the decisive factors defining highly effective and master teachers.[1]

Most states are using instruments like Danielson's and correlating it with student growth on state tests to configure a "numerical" rating of their teachers. On the surface, these instruments seem to make sense. They define what good teaching is, breaking down the four domains into individual indicators. The instruments require a "trained administrator" to go into classrooms and use the instrument with the rubrics to rate what he or she observes for a short amount of time.

These observations take place a few times each school year, often using multiple trained administrators to rate the same teacher, correlating their multiple ratings with student test scores. The correlated scores rank the teacher as highly effective, not effective, or somewhere in between. The scores are also used to drive professional development for a particular teacher in his or her area of weakness as well as determining if there is a common area of concern in a specific area for an individual school.

Using today's advances in technology, all of this recorded and collected data and information can be easily organized and sorted as well as scored for the administrative staff as they use their iPads to record what they "see" during observations.

So what is the problem?

This story and view of teaching and learning is well thought out, includes many useful descriptions of adequate practice, and can be easily downloaded into portable tech devices, defining what good and even distinguished/masterful teaching looks like. The challenging issue that we have with this system is it breaks the task of teaching down into parts, suggesting that if an individual can place enough of these parts together, they will be a great teacher. Underneath this view of teaching is an unstated idea that we can "quantify" excellent teaching and even give it a numerical score, a number. Teaching is not an exact science; it is an art. Teaching is not a job; it is a vocation. Great teaching cannot be quantified because the majority of instruction, connection, assessment, relationships, and communication do not fit into a neatly prescriptive rubric.

If one steps back just a bit, we begin to see a machine or factory model view of teaching and learning, coupled with new technology, but still resting on a foundation that dates back to the Industrial Revolution and has its roots in Prussia. This paradigm or way of seeing what schools and teachers do is embedded within these evaluation models and rubrics. Most, if not all, of these instruments view teaching and learning through a lens that is based on a certain way we interpret schools and schooling.

The challenge with the current view of teaching is that it breaks the art of teaching down into indicators and domains suggesting that accomplishing the twenty-two indicators observed in a 40-60 minute time period, defines a teacher's effectiveness. Does this evaluation system identify master teachers? In this current story, we continue to see the teacher's role as a transmitter of knowledge. This is a false picture of what teaching is and what is required of master teachers. This current story also produces a false and perplexing image of education for children and youth.

*Teaching isn't rocket science; it's harder.*

RYAN FULLER

Rather than continue to break teaching and learning into discrete parts, we need to begin to view teaching and learning as part of a living system. We need to integrate and bring this living system together. Exploring beneath the vocation of teaching we begin to see the art, practice, and craft of teaching. Just as parents envision the dreams and hopes for their own children, we need to envision and re-vision educational opportunities in our classrooms and schools. Human growth is not linear. It is not a process neatly lined up in a step-by-step process. Human growth is a bit messy.

*It [growth] is instead a switchback trail: three steps forward, two back, one around the bushes, and a few simply standing, before another forward leap.*

DOROTHY CORKVILLE BRIGGS

The Inuit people have a wonderful saying, *"There are two plans to be honored every day: My plan and the Mystery's plan."*[2] Anyone who has spent any time in a classroom would recognize the truth beneath this saying. Teaching is an unpredictable and ever flowing interaction between human beings. A teacher can literally plan a lesson for days; yet, no matter how well we plan instruction, dispositions, interactions, and a plethora of other human events can and do impact the lesson. We have all taught planned lessons that we were not very sure would ever work out, and these turned into magical connecting moments! There is an underlying uncertainty in the craft of teaching and learning that makes every day feel like a "high wire act."

Underneath all the various teacher rubrics that describe excellence is an unpredictability and vulnerability that is teaching.

If we are truly concerned with creating a twenty-first-century education for our children, the vision of Stephanie Pace Marshall can begin to assist us to "see" and "think" differently:

*"To educate our children wisely requires that we create generative life affirming learning communities, by design. These communities are grounded in the principles of life and learning and have their roots in: purpose, not prescription; meaning, not memory; engagement, not transmission; inquiry, not compliance; questions, not answers; exploration, not acquisition; personalization, not uniformity; interdependence, not individualism; collaboration, not competition; challenge, not threat; and trust and joy, not fear."*[3]

## MICHAEL & LORI

### *The Story of Well-Being*

#### Purpose Not Prescription

Today our current educational reform model is overly scripted by legislators who have never set foot inside a classroom as a teacher. We have standardized curriculums for each and every grade level, as many teachers are given a script for how to teach a particular standard or sub-standard. This script delivers the correct amount of information to the students. Each curriculum guide has pacing charts that tell teachers how much time to spend on certain skills. These guides are now paced, often by the day, from kindergarten to the twelfth grade. Our schools are more scripted now than at any other time in the history of public education.

What is the purpose of school? We believe the purpose is to live outside the walls of school pondering the questions, understanding the multiple meanings of social, emotional, and cognitive experiences. The paradoxes of learning do not fall inside a rubric and cannot be measured with an instrument. When we return to the purpose of education and its hot, messy, extravagant opportunities, we slowly discover purpose and meaning inside our own lives. This, we feel is a much grander aspect of education.

#### Meaning Not Memory

Human beings naturally learn. Our species would not have survived without this inborn gift. Learning is what we do. We learn when and where we find meaning. Meaning drives human learning, not memorizing disparate uninteresting bits and facts. Currently, our standardized (one-size-fits-all) curriculum leans heavily on memorization, and many of the students we serve are finding less and less meaning in their schoolwork. School becomes meaningful when our expertise, our points of interest, and views are heard and questioned with respect and acceptance. Only then do we try and connect new material and content to what we already know.

## Engagement Not Transmission

Great teachers create engaging experiences, thoughts, and ideas for students to question. Great teachers are engaged with the subjects they teach, and they learn to engage groups of young people, creating learning that is exciting and fun! The current system is relying heavily on transmission of facts in hopes that students can "pass" increasingly higher and higher stakes testing. The pressure to pass these high stakes tests is distorting the teaching and learning process. The pressure felt by teachers and students squelches the creative and innovative habits of mind that create lifelong learners. To engage is to excite, affirm, and appreciate the effort and process of learning. When we focus on the process, we see "success" and students who come to life when they have mastered short-term goals and student-created benchmarks.

## Inquiry Not Compliance

"Inquiry" is defined as "a seeking for truth, information, or knowledge; seeking information by questioning." An old adage states: "Tell me and I forget, show me and I remember, involve me and I understand." The last part of this statement is the essence of inquiry-based learning. Compliant learning involves what many of us did in school, "sit and get." Compliant learning does not involve the learner. The student role in this type of model is to "learn" what the authority says is important to learn. This boils down in the real world to memorization of what one needs to learn in the moment to pass the test. Within a day or two, the content from the assessment is gone from the brain because there was no personal meaning or connection to the material. Inquiry involves the students' abilities to design, ask, and reflect upon questions. Inquiry is student-led.

## Questions Not Answers

Questions drive all learning, yet in our schools we rarely give students much support in learning how to ask great questions.

*Once you have learned how to ask relevant and appropriate questions, you have learned how to learn and no one can keep you from learning whatever you want or need to know.*

NEIL POSTMAN AND CHARLES WEINGARTNER

Currently our schools are very concerned with correct answers. Correct answers drive the system. Our best and brightest students are afraid to make a mistake for fear that their GPAs will be affected, and they will fall back in their class ranking. Our most at-risk youth quickly see school as simply regurgitating correct answers to meaningless questions, dropping out literally or simply going through their educational track half awake. Schools will need to begin to teach how to formulate great questions. This is what drives real learning.

## Exploration Not Acquisition

Creating engaging lessons that begin to spark student

interest and questions, begins with teachers who are able to create instructional tasks that motivate students to desire to know something more! For example, we are teaching students in upper elementary and middle schools about their brains. As we begin to explore the brain with students, they want to know everything! As we have shared our enthusiasm about the power of his or her brain, questions have formed and students of all ages are willing and wanting to explore sleep and the brain, nutrition and the brain, and dreams and the brain. The list goes on and on. Students care about how stress affects their lives. They want to know more about relationships and the brain because this is a living aspect of their worlds. When students feel the relevance in their own lives to a topic or subject, they are doing much more than acquiring information. Acquiring information is not education.

Bloom's Taxonomy was revised in the mid-nineties and now looks like this: Remembering, Understanding, Applying, Analyzing, Evaluating, and at the highest level of the taxonomy is Creating.[4] Our current school systems remain at the remembering and understanding level of Bloom's filter, and the current emphasis on high stakes testing will not encourage movement up this continuum.

## Personalization Not Uniformity

The current standards movement began in 1983 with the publication of *A Nation at Risk: The Imperative for Educational Reform*.[5] This report was completed by President Ronald Regan's National Commission on Excellence in Education. Since that time we have seen a movement by the majority of our states to create curriculum frameworks for all the content areas taught in our schools that identify the specific knowledge or skills the students must acquire by grade level. We are creating tests that will measure how well students acquire that knowledge, instituting high stakes tests for graduation from high schools or to receive a certain level of diploma. This has steered us today to the Common Core Standards for language arts and mathematics currently adopted by forty-three states, the District of Columbia, and four territories.[6] We have created a uniform curriculum guide for language arts literacy and mathematics. Many of the other content areas have been standardized as well. This uniformity as well as the continual testing makes it harder and harder to personalize any content for students. Students march through these curriculum frameworks in a step-by-step manner. Their individual gifts are rarely identified. It is personalization that creates meaning and real learning. Our current push toward uniformity will prepare our students more for the nineteenth century than the stated goal of a twenty-first-century education.

## Interdependence Not Individualism

Although a hallmark of our country has been individualism, it is fairly obvious that our world is becoming smaller and feels more intimately connected. Success in schools, vocations, and communities in the twenty-first century will require the ability to work and live in an interdependent manner. With our current technology, we are literally connecting with one another throughout the world. This will require us to learn to depend on one another and work collaboratively. No one is tested individually in the world. People, companies, families, and marriages all work with the skills of interdependence.

As author Steven Covey stated:

*"Our most important work, the problems we hope to solve, or the opportunities we hope to realize require working and collaborating with other people in a high-trust, synergistic way— whether at home or at work. Having an interdependent mindset, skills and tools are vital, especially now as we work through challenges unlike anything most of us have ever seen in our life time."* [7]

Our current school structure still works in an individualistic and highly competitive fashion. Although collaboration is discussed, it is not the basis of how schools teach, lead, and work with students. All the reward and incentive systems in our schools are generally for individual achievements. The idea of becoming interdependent is just that—an idea. For the most part, our teachers continue to work individually, or, at best, in grade level or content areas with a few common planning times. Rethinking how we can enhance the manner in which we organize teaching and learning will require some experimentation and innovation that the current standards movement stifles. To learn the skills to function in an interdependent manner, we need to refocus our goals and create ways for everyone within a school system to learn to work together. To learn to function in a collaborative manner will require a rethinking of current practices and policies in many areas. In *Collaborating: Finding Common Ground for Multiparty Problems*, Barbara Gray describes collaboration this way:

*"Collaboration is a process through which parties who see different aspects of a problem can constructively explore their differences and search for solutions that go beyond their own limited visions of what is possible."* [8]

The profession of teaching has a history of non-collaboration and isolation. We must learn this skill as we begin to teach the students we serve to flourish with one another in a twenty-first century world. We can begin to create communities of learning, not just for our students but for ourselves.

## Challenge Not Threat

Threats and a continuous stream of negative consequences have been the cornerstones of how we tend to "manage" students in our schools. These coercive practices often carry over into our places of employment. When establishing learning cultures, which rely on trust and cooperation, schools will need to shift from their current reliance on compliance and obedience models toward an emphasis that allows them to build cooperation among all members of the school community. Schools and teachers need cooperation much more than control; yet, we rarely spend time thinking about what generates cooperation. Schools cannot use negative consequences to improve students or teachers. Threatening environments create stress and resistance. High levels of stress literally inhibit and block focus and learning. We cannot threaten or coerce our way to improved and awakened twenty-first-century schools. If we learn to provide challenging sparks to our students that meet some of their basic needs for meaning and connection, we will begin to move in a direction that will challenge our students in positive ways. Fear-based school reform simply will not work for our students or our teachers.

In John Goodlad's *A Place Called School*, he designates boredom as *"a disease of epidemic proportions,"* and wonders, *"Why are our schools not places of joy?"* [9] One rarely hears words like trust, fun, or joy in the current school reform atmosphere in which we live. Trust, fun, joy, and positive connections are evident in any master teacher's classroom and are foundational to creating learning communities of any kind. Harder does not mean better. Rigor can quickly turn into quantity of information for memorization rather than quality and depth of a subject of interest that may lead toward a personal passion. Outside of the institution of learning, human beings learn because it is relevant to what they need to know. Learning gives us pleasure. Schools could become places where students experience learning as pleasurable. Fear shuts down the human brain and learning. Schools must be safe places where children and adults can thrive.

*"School environments, administrative policies, and content expertise do not hold a candle to the gentle 'personal philosophy' that radiates from teachers who create connections and relationships with their students."* [10]

This brief vision, sparked by educator Stephanie Pace Marshall, is a road map for school transformation that would lead us toward schooling that reaches far beyond creating future workers or better test takers. Schools can become the environments that nurture and help to grow the whole child and adolescent, not just a narrow focus on cognition. To truly reimagine what schools could become, we can learn much by collaborating and integrating the work of masters or experts from other fields of study.

For example, according to Angeles Arrien, a cultural anthropologist, we can begin to see through a different lens by using various conceptual filters from other cultures, past and present. Dr. Arrien often wrote and taught about the concept of "walking the mystical path with practical feet." This idea resonates as we think about teaching and being a teacher. In our fast paced modern twenty-first-century culture we have become estranged from our basic human roots. Human beings have always mentored their young. We learn quite naturally as a species. Our ability to learn is the sole reason we have survived. We can learn much from our indigenous past. Dr. Arrien reminds us that among tribal peoples, medicine men, shamans, teachers, or seers are called "change masters."[11]

To begin to "walk this mystical path with practical feet," we can discover some very practical facts about the teaching paradigm. Teachers spend the vast majority of their time with children and youth. The first and most critical element, as one begins his journey towards becoming a master at the craft of teaching, is love. Do you love being around young people? Love is certainly something rarely mentioned in our teacher training institutions or our staff development offerings for practicing teachers; yet, master teachers love spending time and creating learning cultures with young people.

Young people are at the center of our work and they are infinitely more important than the content we are attempting to teach. Many of the finest teachers we have known not only love young people but can also identify the developmental levels of the students they are literally crazy about. The key feature from these master educators is their ability to love unconditionally. The love of the content was not the driving force of their passion. Many teachers who either leave our profession or experience minimal success have entered into the field because they had a passion for a certain content area or discipline. They loved mathematics, a specific science, or a language or history or physical education course and thought it would be great to teach it. These teachers seem very surprised when they encounter groups of students who do not care for the subject they teach. Unintentionally, emotional connections are forfeited as teachers try to transmit the content into their students' minds, which is always a recipe for disaster. In *Man's Search for Meaning,* Viktor E. Frankl postulates:

*"Love is the only way to grasp another human being in the innermost core of his personality. No one can become fully aware of the very essence of another human being unless he loves him. By his love he is enabled to see the essential traits and features in the beloved person; and even more, he sees that which is potential in him, which is not yet actualized but yet ought to be actualized. Furthermore, by his love, the loving person enables the beloved person to actualize these potentialities. By making him aware of what he can be and of what he should become, he makes these potentialities come true."*[12]

I have never met a master of the craft of teaching who did not love the young people he or she spent time with much more than the content he or she was teaching. Love connects and leads us towards a compassionate presence, which pays attention to the well-being of another. This well-being goes well beyond the cognitive and academic domain and includes concern about the social, emotional, and spiritual domain of our students. This is the foundation of the ecology of learning. There is an interdependence and connection between the teacher, the students, and the culture of the classroom and the school. Each classroom and school is as unique as a person's fingerprints and can never be successfully standardized. Beneath the interactions and overt behaviors observed in a classroom, master teachers recognize that deep learning comes slowly, through the recognition of patterns, the creation of personal connections, and the construction of relevant personalized meaning.

Masters of the craft of learning know that love is foundational because it is the only way to access the students' hearts. Indigenous cultures have repeatedly shared with the modern world that there is no learning without the heart. We like to keep in mind what the Lebanese artist, poet, and writer Kahlil Gibran taught: *"Work is love made visible."* This quote is a terrific description of a master teacher's work.

Dr. Arrien's work describes four archetypical patterns that she has discovered in her cross-cultural research. These archetypical patterns can assist us as we begin to explore the path to becoming a master teacher. One of the critical things to remember about this path of teaching and learning is that it never ends. Master teachers are always becoming, and our work is never completed. This perspective of teaching allows the work to be endlessly creative. There is always more to know and learn.

The four universal archetypes that Dr. Arrien writes and speaks about are: The Way of the Warrior or Leader; The Way of the Healer; The Way of the Visionary; and the Way of the Teacher. Dr. Arrien states:

*"The four ways reflect a pervasive belief that life will be simple if we practice four basic principles: Show up or choose to be present, pay attention to what has heart and meaning, tell the truth without blame or judgment, and be open, rather than attached to outcome."* [13]

We have read that it takes approximately ten years, a decade of intense reflective work, to become an "expert" in anything. The craft of teaching at a master's level certainly meets this criterion. Following a rubric, or any teacher evaluation instrument, will not take anyone toward mastery of the craft of teaching. This requires a much different kind of work. We can use the work of Dr. Arrien to deepen how we view teaching.

**The Way of the Warrior or Leader**'s task is to show up and be present. Teachers must learn the art of being present every day with the young people in our classrooms. We must learn to show up, regardless of how we feel or what life experiences we are personally encountering. When we enter our classrooms, we must be able to leave our own baggage at the door and be ready to witness and serve the young people we are responsible for. The Way of the Warrior also involves the proper use of power. Dr. Arrien's work describes three kinds of power that are found universally in all cultures. These powers are presence, communication, and the power of position.[14] Masters of the craft of teaching must learn to integrate and understand all three versions of power. Master teachers must cultivate the power of presence in their classrooms. Every person has a presence and teachers who become masters at their craft cultivate and grow their presence. They do this by treating every one of their students with a high degree of dignity and respect. They treat all of their students, regardless of the way their students are acting or behaving, as sacred beings. They refuse to embarrass or discourage any of their students, working diligently at protecting the connections in their classrooms.

Masters of the craft of teaching have also cultivated their ability to communicate. They learn, over time, to use their words effectively. They choose their words carefully and learn to use words and timing so that when they communicate directives, consequences, or desires, students are more likely to be open to the messages shared. Master teachers also cultivate their ability to truly listen to their students and to hear "beneath" the simple surface behaviors.

Lastly, the master of the craft of teaching learns to demonstrate the power of their position by their willingness to take a stand. Teachers make literally thousands of decisions a day, and this power of position allows us to clearly identify what is important. We use the position of power to protect young people we are responsible for, refusing to use our positional power to coerce others. We implement our positional power to form partnerships with our students and our students' families, as well as the community that our school is embedded within.

**The Way of the Healer** is an archetype that pays close attention to what has heart and meaning. Cross-cultural healers have always recognized that the power of love is the strongest healing force available. Masters of the craft of teaching become incredibly competent at noticing others. They notice small changes in their students, including new sneakers, new sweaters, new hairstyles, as well as moods and dispositions. These teachers recognize the weather their students bring into the classrooms. The healer validates his students' feelings, providing them with a felt sense that they are seen, known, valued, and loved.

Dr. Arrien defines four universal healing tools that include: singing, dancing, storytelling, and story reading, as well as silent rituals.[15] This certainly matches up well with the latest research concerning how our brains learn best. Often science has a way of catching up to our older wisdom ways. Stories are powerful healing tools and strategies. The brain thrives and learns deeply with presented patterns and experiences shared in contextual ways. When we share and weave stories into our content, discipline measures, and ways of classroom engagement, our children and adolescents find relevancy and a personal meaning attached to the created stories.

**The Way of the Visionary** is to tell the truth without judgment or blame. This leads one toward cultivating authenticity. As educator and author Parker Palmer states, *"We teach who we are."* Masters of the craft of teaching become more and more authentic and comfortable with whom they are. As human beings, we create and nurture our authenticity, becoming passionate about bringing our personal visions into the world. Masters of the craft of teaching have a vision of what great teaching and learning environments feel like, working to make that vision a reality in their classrooms. They become proactive in their own learning rather than reactive to what is happening around them. The Way of the Visionary also recognizes that each and every individual is unique. Masters of the craft of teaching know this and adapt their teaching styles and content to the unique learning profiles and needs of every student they touch. Although we as teachers teach groups of students, we must always remember that teaching is ultimately connecting with each unique mind and heart. We do not teach groups. We teach individual, unique, young people. Masters of the craft of teaching know that there are no duplicate human beings and that we cannot standardize the human spirit without damaging or diminishing the spark of hope and creativity in each child or adolescent.

The Way of the Visionary also recognizes that two pathways exist, calling forth meaning for each individual student. One pathway is external and seen. This pathway can be quantifiable. It is the pathway of behaviors, spoken words, and seen interactions and communication. The second pathway is internal and sensed. Currently schools spend very little, if any, time on the internal world of our students. Our students carry on in a world of their own, filled with private logic, biases, beliefs, customs, and cultures. When we teach to the mind and attend to creating focused attention through mindful practices, we give our students the tools and resources to move within to their interior worlds. Educational Neuroscience practices and strategies begin to balance this aspect of our teaching and learning processes. This pathway is qualitative. The master in the craft of teaching gathers both kinds of data, quantitative and qualitative, to assist in modifying his practice as a teacher. The data gathered and the modifications designed with regard to instructional practices, assessment, and engagement center on the educator's practices, not the students' behaviors!

Finally, The Way of the Visionary speaks to encouraging and assisting our students in finding their unique gifts and strengths. Masters in the craft of teaching focus on student strengths rather than spending enormous amounts of time and effort trying to "fix" weaknesses. The Way of the Visionary sees what cannot be seen just yet. We mirror back, to our students we serve, the strengths they possess. Master teachers help students remember and discover their purpose.

The last of the Four-Fold Ways is **The Way of the Teacher**.[16] The way of the teacher is to remain open to outcomes. The master in the craft of teaching learns that we cannot control the outcomes of what we teach, nor can we control what our students do with what they learn.

The master in the craft of teaching must become comfortable with states of not knowing, the mystery of how the perception and design are ingested in each young person's mind and heart. This "allowing" involves a great deal of trust from us, knowing that we have taught, led, and mentored our students to the best of our abilities. If we continue to reflect and grow our own skills, our students will model and remember their purpose and sense of self. They will flourish with time and a bit of space and patience. It is difficult not to want to control everything for the children we serve and teach. Yet deep within, we must trust the unfolding process because the harder we try to "control" everything the less control we actually achieve. Trust is a critical component of becoming a master in the craft of teaching.

The Four-Fold Way, adapted from the work of Dr. Arrien, takes us underneath the current story of teaching and learning. Its potential can lead us on a path to becoming masters in the craft of teaching through presence, openness to the outcomes, shared authenticity, and a desire to see and feel the inner pathway and world of each and every student. The Way of The Teacher calls us to explore and examine our own lives, continually reflecting and improving our practices and dispositions—the wisdom cultivated—as we sit beside our students.

 S P A R K S

**Reappraisal Strategies**

1. *"Negative brain bias."* When we understand how we perceive experiences in negative ways, we relax a bit more

because there is an understanding as to why we are able to create so many negative thoughts throughout the day. Our brains are wired to survive, and this has not changed through the thousands of years of neurobiological development. To survive as a species means we have to pay attention to what we perceive as negative. When our youth understand how our perceptions are challenged with neural biology that leans to the negative side, they are able to shift perspectives with more ease.

The memories we form change too! New research on memory consolidation could be very helpful to students who have experienced ongoing trauma and stress. Each time we recall a memory, our minds innately add, distort, or delete the initial facts as each memory is recalled and consolidated.[17]

What if we were able to self-reflect and share a memory that, over time, is replaced with supplementary positive memories and understandings? As educators we can empower our students with a plasticity of perspective through circles of sharing, five-minute written or drawn reflections, and our own narrative—a shared modeling technique of day to day challenging experiences. Last week in the seventh grade, I did just this. I shared with the students some perceived negative feedback from a colleague as we discussed the power of perspective and memory. I talked about how upset and hurt I had initially felt. Next, I discussed how the words from this co-worker had subtly altered my personal feelings and self-confidence for a day or two. My posture, motivation, and preoccupation with this experience were palpable and negative. But then I chose a couple of effective coping strategies that work for me. I decided to give myself a good "talking to," and also invited a couple of close friends into my dilemma. They were able to listen, and to assist me in reappraising the experience in a way that improved my emotions! I recalled the power of the negative brain bias and how we can obsess over an experience that becomes inflated and distorted by our own brain interpreters—the negative bias team!

2. *Perspective exercise.* Research reports know that writing out our thoughts, anger, anxieties, and negative emotions clears space in the working memory, improving test scores.[18] When we write a letter to ourselves, as if we were giving advice to a friend . . . the objectivity steps in and our brains create a larger perspective while creating space in the working memory. Writing a letter to ourselves, as if we were writing to give advice to a friend in need, is a powerful strategy for stepping outside ourselves, creating options, alternatives, and a lens to see a renewed experience.

3. *Ninety-second rule.* Research from Dr. Jill Bolte Taylor explains that our bodies have the ability to rinse themselves of negative emotion in ninety seconds.[19] But we embrace the capacity to stay angry for days, weeks, and years. Why? The reason we stay angry, afraid, anxious, and upset is that the thoughts we replay over and over again about a particular experience, and the more we replay a thought or experience, the more distorted it becomes. Each time we remember and share a memory, we actually create a new memory because we have subconsciously altered the previous one.

4. *Reward system in the brain—positive peer feedback.* Relationships and social connection are finding their way into

significant research with regard to brain health. Psychologist and author Dr. Matt Lieberman reports:

*"Not only are we attuned and sensitive to positive feedback from others, but our reward systems in the brain respond to such far more strongly than we might have guessed."* [20]

When we sit beside a student and create lists of strengths and interests, we help our students create a renewed focus and problem-solving potential through a strength-based lens. Each week, a group of students, and possibly an adult from outside the classroom, could be appointed to a "wellness" committee. The name of this committee and the number of students involved would be determined by the educator and individual classes. We know that our social aptitudes are present in our biology, but with experiences and feedback they can be strengthened and shared. These individuals would provide a problem-solving resource for students to access. There would need to be predetermined guidelines and agreements by the adults and youth, but with intentional planning and an open mind, this strategy could actually strengthen emotional connections and relationships in the classrooms.

5. *Positive aspects of painful self-reflection.* For the past several semesters, I have asked my students to share a paper entitled, "The Gift." This paper is a self-reflection assignment where students are asked to remember a very painful or negative time in his/her life. The memory of this time is revisited for this assignment, and we discuss current perceptions and ask questions that provoke deeper reflection. What are three possible positive outcomes to this perceived negative experience? We can usually find these with hindsight, but what if we were to begin to focus

on the positive aspects of this experience? How were others affected? How did this change your ideas or thoughts about a past thought or belief? What would you do differently next time? How would this present in a classroom? This spark could be integrated across subject areas and the possibilities of how this strategy could be implemented are vast.

The craft of teaching is an ongoing process that calls us to dive below the surface of the five senses. When we tap into our own deep and fluid intuition, seeing the possibilities in ourselves and in our students, we step onto a path that leads to connections with others. Does feeling more socially connected with others improve academic performance? Dr. Matt Lieberman reports these findings: "A number of studies have now shown a modest impact on GPA of being accepted by other students or feeling more connected to their school."[21] Dr. Lieberman continues to explain:

*"After our journey through the latest research on the social brain, we know that it isn't the students' fault they are distracted by the social world. We are built to turn our attention to the social world because of survival."*[22]

We improved our lives through our evolution because we paid attention to our environments. Our classrooms inside the new story need to turn their attention back to the prolific benefits and natural ways of collaboratively learning because of our innate propensity for social connectedness.

# CHAPTER 7

# The Story of Now
## *No One Else is Coming!*

MICHAEL & LORI

THE FIELD OF EDUCATION is at a threshold. We are moving through a time in educational reform that has taken us into a frantic pace within the current place of "Now." That place is a dead end. This direction of education reform will continue for a little while longer trying to make the current story work. Those who continue to view education as a machine will continue the push for an increase in rigorous standards—more tests and data—holding preschools through colleges and universities accountable for outcomes. It is a system based on finding and correcting deficits, and it is slowly dying. John O'Donohue summarizes the concept of thresholds well in *To Bless the Space Between Us*:

> *Like spring secretly at work within the heart of winter, below the surface of our lives huge changes are in fermentation. We never suspect a thing. Then when the grip of some long-enduring winter mentality begins to loosen, we find ourselves vulnerable to a flourish of possibility and we are suddenly negotiating the challenge of a threshold.*

*At any time you can ask yourself: At which threshold am I now standing? At this time in my life, what am I leaving? Where am I about to enter? What is preventing me from crossing my next threshold? What gift would enable me to do it?*

*A threshold is not a simple boundary; it is a frontier that divides two different territories, rhythms, and atmospheres. Indeed, it is a lovely testimony to the fullness and integrity of an experience or a stage of life that it intensifies toward the end into a real frontier that cannot be crossed without the heart being passionately engaged and woken up. At this threshold a great complexity of emotion comes alive: confusion, fear, excitement, sadness, hope. This is one of the reasons such vital crossings were always clothed in ritual. It is wise in your own life to be able to recognize and acknowledge the key thresholds; to take your time; to feel all the varieties of presence that accrue there; to listen inward with complete attention until you hear the inner voice calling you forward. The time has come to cross.*[1]

We find ourselves at a place and time where we are standing at the boundary of a new frontier. As O'Donohue writes, "It is a time of great "complexity of emotion" that comes alive that includes "confusion, fear, excitement, sadness, and hope." As Barbara Widhalm reminds us, "Educators are architects of living systems."[2]

The threshold that we find ourselves inside of now is one that views learning as alive and vibrant, and we are slowly leaving behind the view of learning as a sterile and dispassionate pursuit. These are exciting times to be involved in our vocation. The time has come to cross the threshold. We can and must release ourselves from the standards-driven idea of schooling. It has proven to be a dead end that leads nowhere and has not had a positive and growth encouraging effect on our children.

As Iris C. Rotberg wrote in the Phi Delta Kappan,

numerous studies show school choice has increased seg-regation of students by race, ethnicity, and socioeconomic status. Sixty years after Brown v. Board of Education, our schools are getting more separate and less equal. School choice is making this worse. Often inside many of the current charter schools that are continuing to expand in America's neediest communities, there is an emphasis on order and control. In many of these schools the emphasis also strives for obedience of adult demands and reflects an environment that relies heavily on the use of rewards and punishments. This is antiquated and contrary to the needs of the twenty-first century.[3]

When it comes to punishment in our schools and classrooms, what societal values and personal theories anchor our culture below the waterline of reason and understanding in this realm of human experience? What thinking errors are implemented to endorse the belief that harsh punishment is effective in fighting defiance and delinquency in our students?[4]

If we step back and reflect on the current charter school movement, it is becoming very clear that this cannot be seen as the answer to the transformation of our schools. There are charter schools that appear to be highly effective, and no doubt we could find students who have thrived in charters after struggling in their neighborhood schools; but overall, the performance of charter schools is highly mixed and often no better than that of neighborhood schools.[5]

The standards, privatization, and accountability movement, started in the 1980s, has run its course. It will not lead our young towards the needed skills and abilities of the twenty-first century. It has failed! The Story of Now will not be a single story. Living systems cannot be standardized no matter how hard we try. The process of change in living systems cannot be directed from the outside but must be provoked from within. The Story of Now will encompass many different stories.

Education and schooling are already beginning to take many different paths and that trend will continue in unpredictable and creative ways. The Story of Now is occurring in pockets within schools and districts all over our country. These changes do not need to begin as radical reforms. They can begin as easily as changing the starting times of our high schools so that we allow our schools to match the biological clocks of the adolescents within them. Currently many schools across our country embrace a collaborative model with teaching staff working together to make learning more relevant in the lives of the students who sit beside them. The Story of Now can be seen in schools that are expanding the offerings to include the arts, music, and dance, as well as the more traditional content area subjects. The Story of Now can be "felt" as one moves within these schools experiencing energy of excitement and aliveness in both the adults and young people.

As we discussed and addressed in chapter four, adverse conditions such as poverty, neglect, abuse, death, divorce, mental illness, or any ambient trauma creates disrupted neural development. We cannot teach in masterful ways without acknowledging these critical interferences in development. A student who has an acute and powerful need for control, power, attention, love, and dignity, oftentimes has reverted and stabilized neural circuitry in the brain that has become hardwired in the stress response state. And these brain states are powerfully reinforced when a student is up against an adult who has stepped inside the conflict cycle, even unintentionally.

Why is it so difficult for these patterns of negative oppositional reactions within the fight/flight response to diminish? We understand that these brain states begin to feel safe, secure, and familiar—and sometimes these feelings are the only permanent interchanges a child or adolescent has experienced or been taught. A child or adolescent may perceive feelings of safety in the midst of trauma. Many children and adolescents, who have not securely attached to an adult in early life, walk into our classrooms and schools mistrusting most adults.

*When a teacher uses total [intentional] positive feedback,*
*he or she will feel calm and in control, which should*
*result in powerful, positive emotional consequences for*
*the teacher and the entire class.*

JOSEPH CIACCIO
IN *HOW TO TEACH THE UNTEACHABLE*

Research shows that the quality of human relationships in schools and youth service programs may be more influential than the specific techniques or interventions employed."[6]

In *Attachment-Based Teaching*, Dr. Louis J. Cozolino writes that teachers should keep four things in mind as they plan their work. First, brains grow best in the context of relationships. Connections matter greatly to school engagement as well as school performance. Second, classroom environments need to be places of low stress levels and emotional arousal. Teachers must orchestrate the emotional tone of their classrooms. Third, there needs to be a balance between the focus on thinking and the focus on feeling. When we teach we must connect to the heart as well as the mind. Finally, teachers need to creatively use stories in their teaching. Stories have been shown to increase memory as well as connecting the mind with the heart.[7]

Another significant story in this time is the refreshing reframing of higher education and career opportunities and options. A traditional four-year degree may not be the singular path for everyone, and the variety of educational /vocational platforms are beginning to be recognized as a welcomed change. Many families in the United States are facing significant levels of poverty, and college debt is a realistic challenge. There are also many students who do not learn in traditional environments, and our culture and students are starting to recognize the unique needs, passions, and opportunities for future social, emotional, and academic growth. This story will continue in unpredictable and creative ways. For example, Coursera is an online educational platform that partners with some of the top universities in the world offering free courses to anyone who wants to take a class.[8]

Other open source platforms are springing up daily. Academic Earth began in 2009 and offers individualized education to anyone in the world from universities such as Carnegie Mellon, Columbia, Cornell, MIT, and many others.[9]

**Unconferences** or open space conferences for teaching and learning have been around for a number of years. At an unconference, people come together at a specific location with an active sign-up on the spot. There are no topics that are pre-planned. There is no keynote speaker, prearranged agenda, or panel discussions. The unconference is formatted based on who attends and who chooses to participate. The participants decide what topics will be discussed at various sessions during the day. The participants create the agenda and the "rule of two-feet" applies. If you are in a session that you find is not of value to you, it is perfectly acceptable to leave and attend another session. If you feel you have something of value to offer the group, you simply sign up as a presenter that day. These conferences rely on the creativity and expertise of who shows up! Imagine what could be if we allowed our students to take one or two school days a year and work alongside their teachers creating and implementing an unconference? What might we learn about our students as we begin to explore their unique strengths and passions?

We are sitting on a new threshold of re-visioning education that offers vast possibilities for our not-too-distant future. The Story of Now will involve a continual moving away from standardization toward increased personalization and the cultivation of our individual human gifts. It will be a move away from competition and comparison toward creating individualized growth and development for our young. It will be a moving away from the idea that we can make our children into the latest and greatest "professions of the day." We see this now in the current push toward making "all" our young people Science, Technology, Engineering, and Math (STEM) professionals. The idea that we can make and brand our children into a specific kind of professional is a dead-end idea, and in our current context, is impossible to predict. In our current context we are preparing our young for work that does not yet exist.

According to Forbes magazine, 91 percent of young people born between 1977 and 1997 will have between fifteen and twenty different jobs over their lifetime. Many of those jobs have not been invented yet![10]

*The future for education is not in standardizing but in*
*customizing, not in promoting groupthink and*
*"de-individuation," but in cultivating the real depth and*
*dynamism of human abilities of every sort.*

KEN ROBINSON
IN *THE ELEMENT: HOW FINDING YOUR PASSION*
*CHANGES EVERYTHING*

The Story of Now will involve a broadening of our view of intelligence. It will ask students a different type of question, modeled by the Learning Disabilities Association of Colorado at the Denver Academy. We have currently focused on the question, "How smart are you?" The new question will ask, "How are you smart?" This independent school that began to ask this question was created for students who learn differently. Its focus is on creating a student profile that focuses on the strengths of the whole student.[11]

Currently our school systems hold a narrow view of human intelligence, recognizing only a small sliver of our human capacities. In our schools now, you are only "smart" if you are word smart or number smart. The Story of Now will broaden this very limited view of human capabilities. Howard Gardner's research and work on multiple intelligences is an ideal conceptual model to expand our limited view of intelligence. Gardner has identified nine different types of intelligence humans have the potential to possess. These include: musical intelligence, naturalist intelligence, logical-mathematical intelligence, existential intelligence, interpersonal intelligence, body-kinesthetic intelligence, linguistic intelligence, intrapersonal intelligence, and spatial intelligence.[12]

We are at the very threshold of a re-visioning of what

intelligence is. We now know that intelligence can be taught. Teachers who use strategies that include instruction in problem solving, metacognition, and strategic thinking have been shown to increase cognitive functioning. Research has demonstrated that intelligence is flexible and subject to change. In other words, brains change themselves through good instructional practices.[13]

Other forms of intelligence have been identified in the work of Daniel Goleman that focuses upon the intersection of cognition and emotions. Goleman's work speaks of the critical importance of educating the emotions, and he suggests that it is as important as educating the mind. Emotional intelligence, as well as social intelligence, is critical to the optimal development of our young.[14]

The Story of Now will have schools intentionally teaching creativity. Creativity is often noted as a twenty-first century skill. Daniel Pink (2005) has written about the need for creative thinking and problem solving in our increasingly interconnected world. Pink believes that the future belongs to humans who have cultivated and developed their creative minds. Pink has identified six human abilities that he believes people will need to be successful. These abilities include: design—moving beyond function to engage a person's senses; story—people learn best by the use of stories; symphony—adding big picture thinking; empathy—engaging the emotions as well as using intuition; play—bringing lightness and humor to our efforts; and meaning—bringing personal purpose to what it is we are doing.[15]

Sir Ken Robinson, Ph.D., is an internationally recognized leader in the development of creativity. He defines creativity as "the process of having original ideas that have value." Creativity, according to Robinson, is about fresh new ways of thinking that also involve making judgments concerning the value of what is being created.

Grant Wiggins, co-author of *Understanding by Design*, recently developed a rubric for assisting teachers in defining and cultivating creativity with their students.[16] This certainly integrates well with the latest version of Bloom's Taxonomy in the cognitive domain. Bloom's Revised Taxonomy has now added "Creating" at the top level of the cognitive domain. Certainly the Story of Now must include the cultivation of creativity in our educational systems.

The Story of Now will have an increasing number of schools implementing the latest research from neuroscience to guide engagement of our students' unique brains and how this research attaches educational meaning, emotion, and relationships in and out of school. The implicit goal of education is to change our children's brains by improving both the knowledge base and their understanding of information through the guidance and direction of their teachers. We now understand that every experience a child encounters, such as a class, an instruction, or an assignment, will structurally and functionally change the brain. This is the best news for educators in this new story. We have been given the scientific research to apply instruction that aligns with attention, motivation, and the stress response that inhibits learning when activated. When an individual perceives a threat to his or her safety, attention shifts to the survival response in the brain. In this survival response, we prioritize our need to feel physically and emotionally safe. The ability to learn, problem solve, emotionally regulate, and pay attention are shut off when the brain is in this mode of reactive survival. The ability to solve a math equation and write a persuasive paragraph is impossible when the prefrontal lobes are shut down and not metabolizing because the stress response is activated. Student and educator stress is vital to understand and address. Inside a living system, human communication, motivation, personalities, values, and cultures continuously collide. The central tenet of the teaching and learning exchange is for the adults in a school system to remain open and receptive. As adults working with young people who may be walking into schools with high levels of toxic stress, we need to recognize that education begins with acknowledging and validating the feelings inside this toxicity that hijacks our fluid thought and emotional processing. We need to prepare educators and students with the tangible resources that first and foremost activate a calming and regulatory effect on the brain.

Positive affect depends on an attuned connection with a well regulated caregiver. In this New Story, we are beginning to integrate educational neuroscience principles and strategies into our classrooms and schools. Below is a description of how we are sitting beside educators, parents, and students in ways that not only enhance the academics, but begins to build resilient brains and growth-oriented mindsets that will address the conceptual needs of the teaching and learning process.

Here are some examples of how we provide those tools.

A. The educators and students are learning collectively about their own neuro-anatomy and how their feelings, thoughts, and behaviors are intimately connected and affected to and by the CEO (the mind) while trickling into the body (emotional, social, and cognitive health). We spend some time understanding that a brain is not a machine. The brain is not outside of us working on automatic. It is a social organ that affects and directs every experience in our days, empowering us and the emotional, academic, and social outcomes of every experience and relationship. We are no longer the victim of our feelings and thought processes, which can lead to a strong sense of autonomy and self-efficacy.

B. Students are exploring how they learn, how stress occurs in their brains, and how their emotions and thoughts affect every moment in their day. They are given specific strategies to help lessen the stress response, emotionally regulate themselves, and learn the skills to empathize with other people. *Focused Attention Practices* explains a critical and very well-received method as we train and mentor the mind for attention and relaxation. These practices help adults care for and support these young people, too. They are a win-win for everyone.

C. Students and teachers are given principles and strategies to assist with creating meaning and relevance to the content and subjects they are taught. They are learning how memory is processed in the brain and how best to engage with the content for sustainable learning. The principles and strategies include neuroplasticity, which is the brain's ability to rewire and reshape itself based on the experiences encountered. We are mentoring teachers and students about the development of executive functions (sustained attention, emotional regulation, planning, organizing, flexibility, goal setting, and metacognition strategies) and how to implement and weave emotion into our instruction as we draw upon the strengths of every student profile.

D. We are implementing metaphors, visualization, analogies, associations, emotions, story chunking, and imagery, which creates brain states of anticipation, curiosity, novelty, and prediction, as we prepare and prime the brain for learning, lowering stress, and improving engagement.

E. The most significant aspect of this professional development inside the Story of Now is the attention and care of the educator's brain! If teachers and administrators are to be transformative, effective leaders and role models in the educational community, they need to employ the knowledge of brain engagement, brain health, and the power of emotional contagion. Educators need to be aware of the significance of mirror neurons and how they can influence the "emotional weather" in their classrooms and schools. Educators must tap into their own hot buttons or triggers, personal stories, and culture to deeply understand how conflict cycles are born and lessened through personal perceptions. The skill of continual self-reflection is what separates effective and superior teachers and administrators. The principles and strategies underlying educational neuroscience will lead us all toward an enriched and growth-producing environment.

The Story of Now is about creating environments within our educational institutions where all children can thrive and reach their full potential. The Story of Now will require us to begin to think and create differently. We must become what we wish to teach.

In their book, *Reclaiming Youth*, Larry Brendtro, Martin Brokenleg, and Steve Van Bockern identify four universal growth needs of all children and youth. They organize those growth needs around a series of four questions:

Am I important to somebody here?

Am I good at something here?

Can I influence my world here?

How can I share my gifts to help others here? [17]

The Story of Now can begin in the present as we answer these four questions for all students that we serve.

# SPARKS

The Story of Now begins with redefining classroom roles and responsibilities so students are given the actual experiences to begin creating feelings of success and motivation.

How do we establish bonds based on commonalities rather than differences in our schools and classrooms, places where feelings of belonging, mastery, autonomy, and purpose intimately impact the learning and instructional process? We suggest that we create classroom responsibilities, tangible roles, and cooperative tasks that position students and teachers for success.

## A. Classroom Professions

Last week as I was driving to one of our large, diverse public elementary schools, to speak with teachers about connection, my mind went to a different realm of classroom structure and function. I began to think differently about what bonding and empathy look like in our classrooms. Traditionally, we give students classroom responsibilities with different jobs (paper passer, line leader, errand runner, etc.), but what if we built relationships and trust through leadership and caregiving roles?

These roles and responsibilities call us to explore an emotional climate in our classrooms that would breed service and compassion. When we engage with one another, feeling the power of our compassion and service, the neural circuitry in the brain shifts, and our "reward system" of dopamine and serotonin sharpens our focus, emotional regulation, and engagement. We prime our brains for deepened learning and social connection.

The following "classroom professions" can change as needed and are presented as guidelines and ideas for exploring and adapting at all grade levels. These class responsibilities and roles are vitally important in secondary education, as well, as we are providing opportunities for our students to experience co-leadership roles rather than being passive recipients of rules, lectures, and dispensed knowledge.

### 1. Giver

This student's responsibility is to give encouragement, affirmation, and acts of kindness throughout the day. The giver may use post-its, create signs, deliver spoken messages, or communicate hopefulness by any means.

### 2. Storyteller

Storytelling could take many forms, such as seeking books to share, or integrating vocabulary or content words into a story. Younger students might create a story with pictures. Older students could work with journal stories or other writing/sharing, turning them into screenplays, or submitting them for publication. Your storyteller may develop an iMovie or blog for the class. He or she could create a class story with classmates' names and school projects, or weave any content into this context for learning standards or subject matter. The brain adheres to stories!

### 3. Noticer

This job is to notice what is going well and right. It is the antithesis to tattling or snitching.

### 4. Kindness Keeper

This student would record all of the kind acts performed throughout the day or week. The kindness keeper reflects on these kindnesses and shares with the class periodically.

### 5. Resource Manager

The resource manager suggests ideas, resources, or ways to solve a problem or locate information, either academically or behaviorally.

### 6. Collaborator

This is one role that could be assigned for acting outside the classroom. Maybe there is another teacher, staff member, or student in the school who needs an emotional, social, or cognitive boost. At department and all-staff meetings, the collaborator would share ideas that promote student-to-teacher or student-to-student relationships, or bridging in- and out-group biases that happen when we only perceive differences.

Enjoy these new roles while collecting the perceptual data through surveys, observations, and feedback from one another as the roles change and modify.[18]

## Understanding and Empathy

Creating emotional connections inspires a sense of belonging and service, elevating feelings of purpose, identity, and positive emotion. When we model for one another what we desire to see with regard to behavior and engagement, the social, emotional, and academic learning deepen and are remembered for the long term.

The Cleveland Clinic has produced a video on empathy, which helps us to better understand the life and feelings of another.[19] Fifth-grade students in a Washington Township school in Indianapolis created a similar video in their school. They recorded students in the halls, classrooms, and other school areas, and placed "thought bubbles" depicting what these children might be thinking or feeling. They shared their documentary with the school and created discussion groups in different grade levels.[20]

## Questions for Thought:

1. What roles could you develop in your classrooms that are MAPS for creating student **mastery**, **autonomy**, and **purpose**?

2. How can we model service through our instruction, assessments, and the culture (emotional and physical design) in our classrooms and schools?

3. What are some small "pay it forward" tasks or initiatives that our students could create for the entire school?

Student Engagement is about four questions that the brain thinks about, explores, and reflects upon.
1. How do I feel?
2. Am I interested?
3. Is this important to me?
4. Can I do this?

Now, how do we build instruction around these four questions? When we involve students in the assessment questions such as those stated above, we begin to collect the perceptual data that builds environments of cooperation and collaboration. We begin to model social connectedness where social rejection is diminished because the input and building blocks for academic, social, and emotional success are created and encouraged by all individuals.

Below is a Brain Aligned Survey created for educators to check in with their practices, dispositions, and student engagement. Superior teaching calls us to continually self-reflect and self-assess. We hope this survey informs and invigorates your teaching practices.

### B. Survey: Is Your School/Classroom Brain Friendly?

Before the brain can attend to cognitive learning, students must feel physically safe and emotionally secure. Emotion is a strong force, and when learners experience strong negative emotions, the limbic system kicks in and shuts down cognitive processing. In other words, "reflex" trumps "reflection" when negative emotions occur.

A positive learning environment increases endorphins in the bloodstream which generates a positive feeling and stimulates the brain's frontal lobe to support memory of the learning objective and of the positive situation. A negative learning environment leads to increased cortisol in the bloodstream which raises the learner's anxiety level, shuts down processing of what it perceives to be low-priority information (the lesson content), and focuses the brain on what it perceives to be high-priority information (the situation causing the stress) so that the stressful situation is remembered rather than the lesson content.

Please read the following survey questions and answer to the best of your ability. "Brain-friendly" describes school cultures, environments, strategies, and techniques that capitalize on the way the human brain learns naturally.

Rate each item for an individual classroom, or according to your perception of the school environment as a whole.

Use the following scale to rate each item:
1. Strongly agree
2. Somewhat agree
3. Somewhat disagree
4. Strongly disagree

### Environments that Create a Sense of Belonging and Attachment:

*All long-term learning takes place in the context of relationships.*

MAURICE ELIAS

1. _____ Adults know students by name and students all know the adults within the school.

2. _____ The school is a safe and secure place.

3. _____Children and youth can get to the school safely and without threat of harm.

4. _____The school intentionally connects children and youth with an adult in the school who serves as a source of support.

5. _____The school provides food, clothing, and other assistance to students living in unstable home environments.

6. \_\_\_\_Everyone in this classroom is treated with high levels of dignity and respect regardless of behavior or attitude.

7. \_\_\_\_Everyone in the classroom seems relaxed, yet alert.

8. \_\_\_\_There are lots of laughter and smiling in this classroom.

9. \_\_\_\_The school intentionally avoids the use of coercion to motivate and discipline young people.

10. \_\_\_\_The school intentionally trains its staff to avoid humiliation, shaming, sarcasm, ridicule, or other forms of attack with regard to students' personality, achievement, or behavior.

11. \_\_\_\_The school intentionally gathers perceptual data about its programs and services from all its constituents, including its students.

### Environments that Create a Sense of Mastery and Achievement:

*Children are defeated by failure. Children who are depressed or angry can literally not learn.*
SANDI REDENBACH

12. \_\_\_\_The school formally teaches social and emotional skills to its students.

13. \_\_\_\_The school intentionally recognizes and uses

each student's unique learning style and recognizes multiple forms of intelligence.

14. _____The school establishes practices that ensure that all students experience success in the classroom and that no one is left to fail and flounder.

15. _____There is lots of movement in this classroom.

16. _____ Students in this classroom are talking about what they are learning.

17. _____Everyone is able to drink water in this classroom when they want it.

18. _____There are many visuals being used for all kinds of learning within this school.

19. _____ Children are being formally taught to visualize at this school. Patterns and conceptual models are used to form connections.

20. _____ Music is being used in this classroom during classwork time.

21. _____ Children are moving and using their bodies to learn content in this school.

22. _____ Classrooms are active and novelty is used to increase engagement, yet students know the routines and procedures. Things are buzzing but not chaotic.

23. \_\_\_\_ Children and youth can demonstrate their mastery of material in a variety of ways that allow them to use their learning styles and strengths.

24. \_\_\_\_ Collaborative groups, as well as independent work, is used throughout the day.

25. \_\_\_\_The school regards—and uses—a student's mistakes simply as opportunities for new learning.

### Environments that create a Sense of Independence and Autonomy:

*When possible, engage and maintain students' attention by providing opportunities for them to set their own pace, select the hook that will connect them to the topic, and have some choice in the way they learn the information.*
JUDY WILLIS, M.D.

26. \_\_\_\_The school recognizes that the primary purpose of evaluating a student's work is to determine what type of instruction or resources that particular student needs next.

27. \_\_\_\_The school provides many developmentally appropriate choices to its students.

28. \_\_\_\_The school emphasizes teaching students about their strengths and their gifts through the use of "strength-discovering" assessments.

29. \_\_\_\_The school offers an array of electives for all stu-

dents, and every student can find something they enjoy doing at school.

30. ____The school encourages developmentally appropriate risk taking and discourages a focus on simply taking courses and ranking students by grades and GPAs.

31. ____When teaching, the school staff recognizes that learners ask two critical questions prior to learning for long-term memory: (1) Do I understand it? and (2) What's it got to do with me?

### Environments that Create a Sense of Generosity and Altruism:

*Our higher needs include making full use of our gifts . . . Such needs are fulfilled in an atmosphere of the five "A"s by which love is shown: Attention, Acceptance, Appreciation, Affection, and Allowing.*
DAVID RICHO

32. ____The school provides a menu or opportunities to allow students to experience serving others.

33. ____The school provides a sense of optimism and hope through established rituals that involve all students.

34. ____The school culture emphasizes and demonstrates caring, kindness, empathy, and compassion to all its members. It extends these to the outside community in a variety of ways.

35. \_\_\_\_ The school culture promotes wellness in body, mind, and spirit.

## C. **Abraham Maslow's Hierarchy of Needs Comes to Life in the Classroom!**

In the mid-1950s, humanistic psychologist Abraham Maslow created a theory of basic, psychological, and self-fulfillment needs that motivate individuals to move consciously or subconsciously through levels, or tiers, based on our inner and outer satisfaction of those met or unmet needs. As a parent and educator, I find this theory eternally relevant for students and adults, especially in our classrooms. After studying it over the past couple of years, my graduate and undergraduate students have decided that every classroom should display a wall-sized diagram of the pyramid, as students and teachers alike place pins and post-its on the varying tiers based on their own feelings, behaviors, and needs. What do actual brain-compatible strategies look like on this pyramid?

### Tier One
*Meeting Physiological Needs in the Classroom*

1. **Water bottles and water breaks.**

2. **Focused attention practices.** These practices, involving breathing, imagery, and sound, last one and one-half to two minutes as students close their eyes or focus on an object of attention, practicing quieting their minds from the free-flowing thoughts that bombard their thinking every day.

3. **Physical surroundings.** These include room arrangement, color, temperature, plants, etc.

4. **Food.** Provide a mixed snack bar and have the class designate times to grab some energy bites and continue working.

5. **Instrumental Music.**

These elements contribute to brain-compatible learning by creating a physical environment that is inviting, warm, and friendly!

> *Questions to Ask Myself*
> 1. What do I need?
> 2. Am I tired?
> 3. Am I hungry?
> 4. How much water have I had over the past 24 hours? Is it enough?
> 5. What resources (people, activities, or experiences) could assist me in reaching my small and larger physiological and psychological goals?

## Tier Two
*Stability, Safety and Security, Freedom from Fear*

1. **Attitude.** Sometimes it is enough to have a personal affirmation that creates feelings of safety and security. For example: "Right now in this moment I am safe. I am breathing, I am aware, awake, and I can think and feel!"

2. **Worry drop box.** As you enter the room, drop a written concern in a box situated by the door. Research shows that writing out our concerns and worries frees up the working memory and relieves anxiety.

3. **Pin-ups.** The class assigns various students to physically post a compliment or affirmation each day. We all need to feel validated and often lose sight of our strengths and talents because the brain is wired with a negative bias. These pin-ups help us focus on positive experiences and behaviors instead of faults and mistakes.

4. **Common experiences.** Develop class guidelines together. Create a class blog. Invite outside speakers who promote service and safety: police officers, counselors, former students who have risen above difficult situations, etc.

## Tier Three
*Belonging and Love*

1. **Classroom service project.**

2. **Partnered work.**

3. **Celebrations.** Create special and celebratory days all year long: birthdays, VIP days, strength days, progress days, colorful days, etc.

4. **Working together.** Assign these roles within the class:

- Listener

- Recorder of feelings and thoughts

- Small group of decision-makers

- Student who "cares for" the teacher, office staff, and other students

- Poetry reader

- Designer of classroom decorations

- Gatekeeper who checks for disputes and conflicts

5. **Community circle.** For 3-10 minutes at the beginning and ending of class, share a time where empathy is defined, discussed, and brought to life. You might also share movie clips, personal narratives, or a story to jumpstart the day.

6. **Identity.** A classroom theme, flag, song, flower, and animal totem.

> *Questions to Ask Myself*
> 1. How do I handle negative situations? When these situations occur, what do I typically say to myself?
> 2. What statement would encourage me?
> 3. What are three negative emotions I feel most often?
> 4. What are three positive emotions I feel often or sometimes?

### Tier Four
*Achievement, Recognition and Respect of Mastery, Self-Esteem*

For students to feel capable and successful, we must create an environment that lends itself to this type of mastery.

1. **Expert Day.** Students get to demonstrate personal expertise.

2. **Career Day.** Bring in college students and community members to share the possibilities of academic and professional success following high school.

3. **Display skills as a class.** Create and design quizzes, assignments, and instruction for students in other classes and grades.

*Small Goals I Am Mastering*

1. Completed assignments
2. Dialogued about frustrations
3. Stayed focused on assignments
4. Showed respect and compassion for others
5. Regrouped and continued to work after a frustrating time
6. Helped another student or teacher
7. Contributed ideas and suggestions to a conversation
8. Used positive language in describing a need or desire
9. Self-reflected about my daily work and interactions

*Questions to Ask Myself*

1. What statement would encourage me?
2. Who are my heroes? What character traits do I admire that make them my heroes?
3. How will I know I am on the right track? How will I identify and follow my intuition when it tells me I am straying from pursuing my goals?
4. What are my strengths?
5. What are my challenges?
6. How will I focus on these strengths knowing that my thoughts and feelings drive all my words and actions?

## Tier Five
### *Self-Actualization and Self-Fulfillment Needs*

This level is self-evaluation related to service. We begin to explore and model for our students how to design, evaluate, and analyze information outside of our own basic needs. In this tier, serving others becomes a priority. When we self-assess, we begin to observe how individual perspectives can distort or strengthen our experiences and relationships. Are students able to perceive another view of a situation that would help them to imagine and feel the feelings of a fellow human being when something pleasant or unpleasant happens? A classmate? A teacher? A friend?

Traditionally we were taught that to place all others and their needs above ourselves is a recipe for goodness and well-being, but is this accurate? If students walk into classrooms and schools feeling diminished and negative, they have very little positive emotion and effective collaboration to give to others. This explains why, as teachers, we must model altruism for students to help them understand, and not assume they have learned empathy at home. Many have not.

To become creative thinkers, we have to discover the problem, not just come up with a solution. In this tier, students become self-assessors and self-reflectors. They are able to see and understand how their actions, thoughts, and feelings affect all lives.

*Questions to Ask Myself*
1. What is my purpose in life?
2. What are the challenges in reaching my purpose and the lives of others?

3. How can I serve the world?
4. Why is there conflict and war? What can I do?
   What can we do? [21]

We began this last chapter with the idea that our current story of education is at a "threshold." We are privileged to be learning and teaching in this era. It is a time of great upheaval as a new way is waiting to be birthed, yet it can no longer be contained. The New Story has already begun, and it will not be stifled nor held back. It will continue to move forward with incremental sustainable changes occurring within the hearts and minds of each student, educator, parent, and school.

*It is time to cross over this threshold into a new
and as yet unexplored world
that will allow all our children to thrive.*
JOHN O'DONOHUE

*Nothing changes if nothing changes.*
LORI DESAUTELS

# EPILOGUE

*Whatever your walk of life, race, or class,*
*you have the right and duty*
*to shake this world*
*with a new dream,*
*because the world is waiting for a new dream.*

GRACE LEE BOGGS
NINETY-NINE-YEAR-OLD CIVIL RIGHTS ACTIVIST

## MICHAEL & LORI

WE HAVE EXHAUSTED ourselves trying to fix and remediate schools and the human beings within them. Focusing on weaknesses and deficits has led us down the path toward despair and hopelessness.

The vocation of teaching, at its very core, is an act of hope and optimism. As our world becomes smaller and smaller, and we become increasingly connected with everyone in our world, it is time to begin to act on our unfolding new vision of education.

Schools are living systems and living systems contain within themselves their own solutions. Schools are alive, and we are working, not as standardized machines, but within webs of human relationships and connections. As Margret Wheatley suggests, in order to make a living system healthier, we need to simply connect it more to itself. Schools and organizations change and grow not by "planned disruptions" or forced coercive practices, but by networks of relationships and connections among people who share a common vision of what is possible. These relationships and networks can be cultivated and grown into healthy communities of practice. These communities can share information, knowledge, and wisdom with one another in formal and informal ways. In living systems, healthy change does not occur through another strategic plan. In living systems, healthy change happens through emergence. Human learning is social and comes to life in close connected relationships. Deep learning is profoundly relational.[1]

So, where do we go from here? Lori and I will leave you with a quote from Stephanie Pace Marshall:

*"Mind shaping is World Shaping. When we change the story, we change the map. When we change the map, we change the landscape. When we change the landscape, we change our experiences and our choices. When we change our experiences and choices, we can change our mind. And when we change our mind, we can change the world."*[2]

As we have completed and reflected upon this story with its accumulation of shared experiences within the schools, with teachers, students, and classrooms, we have grown weary of the words: standardization, reform, rigor, and fidelity. These words describe machines more than human beings who are learning, growing, and changing every day.

## LORI

Just as we rarely speak of the deep pain and fear in children and youth that are hidden beneath so many behaviors that offend and defy us, very few of us speak of the lack of early intimacy and connection that precedes the development of perceived offensive behaviors and dispositions. A re-visioning of educational reform calls for a new description that pays close attention to the social bonds and emotional connections between our youth and ourselves, allowing us to crack the code of pain-based living. In this new description, our priorities, as educators and community members, are to build and create ecologies where children's bio-social needs are met. When we pay attention and begin to understand how cultures of discord create fear, aggression, and sometimes a paralysis of self-reflection and healthy thought processes, we begin to meet the child and adolescent where they are and begin again! "Attachment to adults is a prerequisite to learning from them."[3]

If education means "to lead out," how do we lead our children out into the world equipped with the creative and joy-filled emotional, social, and cognitive well-being they will need?

Where is the joy? I feel the joy begins when we are sharing a presence with our students—accepting their personhood and not simply tolerating their surface behavior! When any of us feel a sense of emotional connectedness, we begin to flourish and step onto the path of thriving.

When children and adolescents walk into our classrooms carrying in their private logic, histories, beliefs, and cultures, I am always amazed at my own "learning" that each student provokes. We don't initially need a strategy, a technique, or plan of action with children who sometimes mistrust adults and life. First we need to be present, to notice, to listen as we feel our way around the landscape of the child. When an emotional connection is felt, we can then begin to ask, "How may I serve you?"

From the words of University of Michigan professor Bill Morse (1915-2008), a leader and pioneer in the field of education, who has worked with challenging youth for over sixty years, *"If you don't recognize that you might have ended up like the most troubled young person you know, leave this work, as your lack of empathy renders you useless."*

*"However we treat the child, the child will treat the world."*
PAM LEO
AUTHOR OF *CONNECTION PARENTING*

We are honored to share this story with you as all of our stories continue developing, unfolding, and changing with each new experience and relationship. Please feel free to contact us at any time with your stories, thoughts, connections, questions, and experiences. Our learning never ceases, and we look forward to new stories that will change brains and hearts—for a world that speaks to the "whole child, adolescent, and adult."[4]

# NOTES

## Chapter One: The System Story

[1] Janie Scull and Amber M. Winkler, "Shifting Trends in Special Education," The Thomas B. Fordham Institute (May 2011), http://www.edexcellencemedia.net/publications/2011/20110525_Sh iftingTrendsinSpecialEducation/ShiftingTrendsinSpecialEducation.pdf.

[2] Ron Miller, "Educational Alternatives: A Map of the Territory," *Paths of Learning*, no. 20 (Spring, 2004).

[3] Emily Richmond, "High School Graduation Rate Hits 40-Year Peak in the U.S.," *The Atlantic* (June 2013), http://www.theatlantic.com/national/archive/20-13/06/high-school-graduation-rate-hits-40-year-peak-in-the-us/276604/.

[4] Ethan Yazzie-Mintz, "Charting the Path from Engagement to Achievement: A Report on the 2009 High School Survey of Student Engagement," http://ceep.indiana.edu/hssse/-images/HSSSE_2010_Report.pdf.

[5] Stephanie Pace Marshall, *The Power to Transform: Leadership That Brings Learning and Schooling to Life*, (San Francisco: Jossey-Bass, 2006).

[6] Mathew Lieberman, "The Social Brain and its Superpowers," YouTube video, from a talk filmed September 19, 2013, posted by TEDx Talks, October 7, 2013, http://www.youtube.com/-watch?v=NNhk3owF7RQ.

[7] Thomas L. Hanson and Gregory Austin, *Student Health Risks, Resilience, and Academic Performance in California: Year 2 Report, Longitudinal Analyses* (Los Alamitos, CA: WestEd, 2003), https://chks.wested.org/resources/APIreportY2.pdf.

[8] Children's Defense Fund, "Each Day in America," January 2014, http://www.childrensdefense.org/library/state-of-americas-children/documents/2014-SOAC_each-day-in-America.pdf.

[9] Saki Knafo, "1 In 3 Black Males Will Go To Prison In Their Lifetime, Report Warns," Black Voices, *Huffington* Post, October 4, 2013, http://www.huffingtonpost.com/2013/10/04/racial-disparities-criminal-justice_n_4045144.html.

[10] Deborah Stipek and Michael Lombardo, "Holding Kids Back Doesn't Help Them," *Education Week*, July 14, 2014, http://www.ed-week.org/ew/articles/2014/05/21/32stipek.h33.html.

[11] Larry K. Brendtro, Arlin Ness, and Martin Mitchell, *No Disposable Kids* (Bloomington, IN, National Educational Service, 2005), 11.

[12] Cindy Kiro, "Ngamatua–Maori parenting–Parenting in tradition and history," *Te Ara, The Encyclopedia of New Zealand*, updated May 27, 2013, http://www.TeAra.govt.nz/en/nga-matua-maori-parenting/page-1.

[13] George Reavis, "The Animal School," Climbing Every Mountain (January 13, 2014), http://climbingeverymountain.com/the-animal-school-inclusion-differentiated-instruction/.

[14] Tracy Kidder, *Among School Children* (Boston: Houghton Mifflin, 1989), 313.

[15] Sobonfu E. Some, *Welcoming Spirit Home: Ancient African Teachings to Celebrate Children and Community*, (Novato, CA: New World Library,1999).

## Chapter Two: The Story of the Educator

[1] Daniel Seigel, *Mindsight* (New York: Bantam Books, 2010), 10, 17.

[2] Nicholas J. Long et al., *Conflict in the Classroom: Successful Behavior Management Using the Psychoeducational Model*, 7th ed. (Austin, TX, PRO-ED, INC., 2014).

[3] David Brooks, *New York Times*, January 23, 2014, http://www.ny-times.com/2014/01/24/opinion/brooks-it-takes-a-generation.html?_r=0.

[4] David A. Sousa et al., *Mind, Brain and Education* (Bloomington, IN: Solution Tree Press, 2010), 11, 69.

[5] Dan Goleman, *Emotional Intelligence* (New York: Bantam Books, 1995), 97.

[6] Bonnie Benard, "Fostering Resiliency in Kids," *Educational Leadership* 51, no. 3 (November 1993): 44–48.

[7] E. Werner and R. Smith, *Vulnerable But Invincible: A Longitudinal Study of Resilient Children and Youth* (New York: Adams, Bannister, and Cox, 1989), 162.

[8] Larry Brendtro and Scott Larson, "The Resilience Code: Finding Greatness in Youth," *Reclaiming Children and Youth* 12, no. 4 (Winter 2004): 197.

[9] William E. Krill Jr. and Marjorie McKinnon, *Gentling: A Practical Guide to Treating PTSD in Abused Children*, 2nd ed. (Ann Arbor, MI: Loving Healing Press, 2009), 1–2.

[10] David Richo, *How to Be an Adult in Love, Letting Love in Safely and Showing it Recklessly* (Boston: Shambhala Publications, 2013), 6–9.

[11] Belinda Williams et al., "Turnaround Teachers and Schools by Bonnie Bernard," in *Closing the Achievement Gap: A Vision for Changing Beliefs and Practices*, 2nd ed. (Alexandria, VA: Association for Supervision and Curriculum Development, 2003).

## Chapter 3: The Student's Story

[i] Michael A. Scaddan, *40 Engaging Brain Based Tools for the Classroom* (Thousand Oaks, CA: Corwin Press, 2008), 64.

## Chapter 4: The Story of Emotions

[1] John Medina, *Brain Rules* (Seattle, WA: Pear Press, 2008), 172–174.

[2i] Larry K. Brendtro and Scott J. Larson, *The Resiliency Revolution. Discovering Strengths in Challenging Kids* (Bloomington, IN: Solution Tree Press, 2006), 3–31.

[3] Nicholas J. Long, *The Conflict Cycle Paradigm: How Troubled Students Get Caring Teachers Out of Control* (Austin, TX, PRO-ED, INC., 2014), 69–90.

[4] Jane Bluestein, *Creating Emotionally Safe Schools, A Guide for Educators and Parents* (Deerfield Beach, FL: Healing Communications, 2001), 147.

[5] Dan Seigel, *Brainstorm: The Power and Purpose of the Teenage Brain* (New York: Penguin Group, 2013), 67.

[6] Ibid.

[7] Ibid., 8.

[8] Nicholas J. Long, Mary M. Wood, and Frank A. Fecser, *Life Space Crisis Intervention, Talking With Students in Conflict*, 2nd ed. (Austin, TX, PRO-ED, INC., 2001), 134.

[9] Carol Dweck, *Mindset, The New Psychology of Success* (New York: Ballantine Books, 2006), 6–7.

[10] The Dalai Lama and Howard Cutler, *The Art of Happiness in a Troubled World* (New York: Doubleday Religion, 2009), 272.

[11] Nicholas J. Long, Frank A. Fecser, and Signe L. Whitson, *Turn Crisis Situations into Learning Opportunities,* Training Manual from Life Space Crisis Intervention Training, developed by the Life Space Crisis Intervention Institute, Hagerstown, MD. (This manual is accessible only to Master and Senior Trainers of the Life Space Crisis Intervention Institute, http://www.lsci.org/).

[12] Paul C. Gorski, *Reaching and Teaching Students in Poverty: Strategies for Erasing the Opportunity Gap* (Multicultural Education) (New York: Teachers College Press, 2013).

[13] Lori Desautals, "Self Assessment Rubric for Social and Emotional Development, Edutopia: Edutopia®, Schools That Work™, Lucas Learning™, and Lucas Education Research™, August 13, 2014, http://www.edutopia.org/blog/self-assessment-inspires-learning-lori-desautels.

## Chapter 5: The Story of Active Hope

[1] 1.  Nicholas J. Long et al., "How To Be a Turnaround Teacher by Bonnie Benard," in *Conflict in the Classroom: Positive Staff Support for Troubled Students*, 6th ed. (Austin, TX PRO-ED, INC., 2007), 635.

[2] Shelley E. Taylor et al., "Biobehavioral Responses to Stress in Females: Tend-and-Befriend, Not Fight-or-Flight,"in *Psychological Review* 107, no. 3 (2000): 411–429.

[3] Nicholas J. Long, Mary M. Wood, and Frank A. Fecser, *Life Space Crisis Intervention, Talking With Students in Conflict*, 2nd ed. (Austin, TX, PRO-ED, INC., 2001), 123.

[4] John Herner, "Discipline: To Teach or to Punish?" *Counterpoint* (Winter 1998).

[5] Nel Noddings, "Schools Face Crisis in Caring," *Education Week* (December 1988): 32.

[6] Lev S. Vygotsky, "Interaction Between Learning and Development" in *Mind in Society*. Translated by M. Cole. Cambridge, MA: Harvard University Press, 1978, 79–91.

[7] Larry K. Brendtro, Martin L. Mitchell, and Herman J. McCall, *Deep Brain Learning, Pathways to Potential with Challenging Youth* (Albion, MI: Starr Commonwealth, 2009), 46.

[8] Merrill Harmin, *Strategies to Inspire Active Learning* (Edwardsville, IL: Inspiring Strategy Institute, 1995), 49.

[9] Thomas J. Sergiovanni, *Strengthening the Heartbeat: Leading and Learning Together in Schools* (San Francisco: Jossey-Bass, 2005), 78.

[10] Henna Inam, "The Power Of Oprah Is The Power Of Questions," Forbes Leadership, July 30, 2013, http://www.forbes.com/sites/hennainam/2013/07/30/why-oprah-is-worth-2-8-billion-the-power-of-questions/.

[11] Jessica Minahan and Nancy Rappaport, *The Behavior Code: A Practical Guide to Understanding and Teaching the Most Challenging Students* (Cambridge, MA: Harvard Educational Press, 2012).

[12] Lisa D. Delpit, *Other People's Children: Cultural Conflict in the Classroom* (New York: The New Press, 1996), 199.

[13] Stephen R. Covey, *The 7 Habits of Highly Effective People*, (New York: Simon & Schuster, 1989), 241.

[14] Ibid., 235.

### Chapter 6: The Story of Well-Being: *The Way of the Teacher*

[1] Charlotte Danielson, "2013 Framework for Teaching Evaluation Instrument (aligned to the INTASC standards)." https://danielsongroup.org/framework/.

[2] Angeles Arrien, "My Plan and Mystery's Plan." Audio interview, IONS Institute of Noetic Sciences, accessed June 4, 2015, http://www.noetic.org/library/audio-interviews/angeles-arrien-intention/#transcript.

[3] Stephanie Pace Marshall, *The Power to Transform: Leadership That Brings Learning and Schooling to Life* (San Francisco: Jossey-Bass, 2006).

[4] Rex Heer, "A Model of Learning Objectives, based on *A Taxonomy for Learning, Teaching and Assessing: A Revision of Bloom's Taxonomy of Educational Objectives*, by L. W. Anderson et al. (New York: Longman, 2001). Iowa State University Center for Excellence in Learn-

ing and Teaching; website updated January 2012. http://www.celt.iastate.edu/teaching-resources/effective-practice/revised-blooms-taxonomy/.

[5] "A Nation at Risk: The Imperative for Educational Reform," April 1983, National Commission on Excellence in Education, last modified October 7, 1999, http://www2.ed.gov/pubs/NatAtRisk/index.html.

[6] Common Core—State Standards Initiative. Preparing America's Students for College & Career. http://www.corestandards.org/.

[7] *FranklinCovey Blog*, "Managing Fear and Insecurity," blog entry by Stephen Covey, June 26, 2009, http://www.franklincovey.com/blog/managing-fear-insecurity.html.

[8] Barbara Gray, *Collaborating: Finding Common Ground for Multiparty Problems* (San Francisco: Jossey-Bass, 1989), 5.

[9] John I. Goodlad, *A Place Called School* (New York: McGraw-Hill, 1984), 242.

[10] Lori L. Desautels, *How May I Serve You?* (Indianapolis, IN: Revelations in Education, 2012), 5.

[11] Angeles Arrien, *The Four-Fold Way. Walking the Paths of the Warrior, Teacher, Healer, and Visionary* (San Francisco: Harper, a Division of HarperCollins, 1993).

[12] Viktor E. Frankl, *Man's Search for Meaning* (Cutchogue, NY: Buccaneer Books, 1959, 1962, 1984, 1992), 134.

[13] Arrien, *The Four-Fold Way*, 7–8.

[14] Ibid., 22.

[15] Ibid., 54.

[16] Ibid., 109–128.

[17] Greg Miller, "How Our Brains Make Memories," *Smithsonian Magazine*, May 2010, accessed June 4, 2015. http://www.smithsonianmag.com/science-nature/how-our-brains-make-memories-14466850/?no-ist=&fb_locale=en_GB&page=6.

[18] William Harms, "Writing about Worries Eases Anxiety and Improves Test Performance," on the website of the University of Chicago. http://news.uchicago.edu/article/2011/01/13/writing-about-worries-eases-anxiety-and-improves-test-performance. (See more at: http://news.uchicago.edu/article/2011/01/13/writing-about-worries-eases-anxiety-and-improves-test-performance#sthash.bwmnXBHI.dpuf).

[19] Jill Bolte Taylor, "The Neuroanatomical Transformation of the Teenage Brain," video recording at TEDxYouth@Indianapolis, January 26, 2013, posted on YouTube, February 21, 2013. https://www.youtube.com/watch?v=PzT_SBl31-s.

[20] Matthew Lieberman, *Social: Why Our Brains Are Wired to Connect* (New York: Broadway Books, 2014), 78.

[21] Ibid., 282.

[22] Ibid.

## Chapter 7: The Story of Now

[1] John O'Donohue, *To Bless the Space Between Us, A Book of Blessings* (New York: Doubleday, 2008), 48.

[2] Barbara Widhalm, "Educators as Architects of Living Systems: Designing Vibrant Learning Experiences Beyond Sustainability and Systems Thinking," *The Journal of Sustainability Education* 2, (March 2011): http://www.jsedimensions.org/wordpress/content/educators-as-architects-of-living-systems-designing-vibrant-learning-experiences-beyond-sustainability-and-systems-thinking_2011_03/.

[3] Iris C. Rotberg, "Charter Schools and the Risk of Increased Segregation," March 27, 2014, http://www.edweek.org/ew/articles/2014/02/01/kappan_rotberg.html.

[4] Larry K. Brendtro and Nicholas J. Long, "Punishment Rituals: Superstition in an Age of Science," *Reclaiming Children and Youth: Journal of Emotional and Behavioral Problems* 6, no. 3 (Fall 1997): 130–135.

[5] Steve Hinnefeld, "An Open Letter to Condoleezza Rice," School Matters: K-12 Education in Indiana, posted on March 12, 2015, https://inschoolmatters.wordpress.com/2015/03/12/an-open-letter-to-condoleezza-rice/#more-5941.

[6] Larry K. Brendtro, Martin Brokenleg, and Steve VanBockern,

*Reclaiming Youth At Risk: Our Hope for the future* (Bloomington, IN, National Educational Services, Revised Edition 2002), 71.

[7] Louis Cozolino, *Attachment-Based Teaching* (New York, W.W. Norton & Company, Inc., 2014), 35.

[8] coursera's website, accessed June 9, 2015, https://www.coursera.org.

[9] ACADEMIC EARTH's website, accessed June 9, 2015, http://academicearth.org/.

[10] Jeanne Meister, "Job Hopping is the 'New Normal' for Millennials: Three Ways to Prevent a Human Resource Nightmare," Forbes Leadership, August 14, 2012, http://www.forbes.com/sites/jeannemeister/2012/08/14/job-hopping-is-the-new-normal-for-millennials-three-ways-to-prevent-a-human-resource-nightmare/.

[11] "How Are You Smart? What Students with Learning Disabilities are Teaching Us," YouTube instructional video, created by the Learning Disabilities Association of Colorado (2008) in partnership with Denver Academy, published October 16, 2012, https://www.youtube.com/watch?v=OdqaUcq7YVQ.

[12] Howard Gardner, "The Nine Types of Intelligence," From: Overview of the Multiple Intelligences Theory, Association for Supervision and Curriculum Development and Thomas Armstrong.com, http://skyview.vansd.org/lschmidt/-Projects/The%20Nine%20Types%20of%20Intelligence.htm.

[13] Arthur L. Costa and Bena Kallick, eds., *Learning and Leading with Habits of Mind,* (Alexandria, VA: Association of Supervision and Curriculum Development (ASCD), 2008), 9.

[14] Daniel Goleman, *Working With Emotional Intelligence* (New York: Bantam Books, 1998).

[15] D. H. Pink, *A Whole New Mind* (New York: Riverhead Books, 2005).

[16] "My reply to Willingham, Part 2," *Granted, and... ~* thoughts on education by Grant Wiggins, Grant Wiggins' Blog, accessed June 9, 2015, https://grantwiggins.files.wordpress.com.

[17] Martin Brokenleg and Steve Van Bockern, "The Science of Raising Courageous Kids," *Reclaiming Children and Youth* 12:1 (Spring 2003): 22–27, https://reclaimingjournal.com.

[18] Lori Desautels, "New Class Roles: Building Environments of Cooperation," Edutopia, December 18, 2014, http://www.edutopia.org/blog/new-roles-building-environments-cooperation-lori-desautels.

[19] "Empathy: The Human Connection to Patient Care," YouTube video, CEO Toby Cosgrove shared this video with the Cleveland Clinic staff during his 2012 State of the Clinic address, published on February 27, 2013, https://www.youtube.com/watch?v=cDDWvj_q-o8.

[20] Lori Desautels, "Empathy," Fox Hill Elementary School - The Brainy Bunch - 2014-2015, YouTube video, Music: "The Giving" by Michael W. Smith (Google Play · AmazonMP3 · iTunes), Published on January 8, 2015, https://www.youtube.com/-watch?v=JKnd2JBARRw.

[21] Lori Desautels, "Addressing Our Needs: Maslow Comes to Life for Educators and Students," Edutopia, February 6, 2014, http://www.edutopia.org/blog/addressing-our-needs-maslow-hierarchy-lori-desautels.

### Epilogue

[1] Margaret Wheatley and Deborah Frieze, "How Large Scale Change Really Happens—Working with Emergence," *The School Administrator* (Spring, 2007).

[2] Stephanie Pace Marshall, A Guide to *The Power To Transform: Leadership That Brings Learning and Schooling to Life* (San Francisco: CA, Jossey-Bass Publishers, Inc., A Wiley Imprint, 2006).

[3] Larry K. Brendtro, Martin L. Mitchell, and Herman J. McCall, *Deep Brain Learning: Pathways to Potential with Challenging Youth* (Albion, MI: Starr Commonwealth, 2009), 19.

[4] Ibid., 6.

# LORI'S ACKNOWLEDGEMENTS

Writing this book has been a journey I will cherish forever. Michael McKnight, thank you for saying "yes" two years ago as we joined experiences, hearts, and minds sharing our life's work through *Unwritten, The Story of a Living System*. This book could not have been created without the support, guidance, and personal investment from the Washington Township District led by Dr. Nikki Woodson. These teachers and administrators willingly welcomed me into their classrooms and schools as a co-teacher during the past two years. Sarah, Deanna, Shawn, Rachel, Emily, Noah, Stacie and Ryan I am forever grateful!

I could not have written these chapters without the Pike Township educators led by Superintendent Nate Jones, who have been so supportive, excitedly integrating these educational neuroscience practices and strategies into their classrooms throughout the district. I also want to acknowledge Lawrence Township in Indianapolis led by Dr. Shawn Smith who has embraced these practices and new discipline with excitement and growing enthusiasm.

Marian University has gifted me with the flexibility and encouragement allowing and supporting my return to the classrooms while sharing these practices with undergraduate and graduate students each week.

There are moments and people who truly impact your work leaving you wordless and very grateful! Thank you to Tom Oestreich and Mary Kay Hunt who always believed in these principles, strategies and the genius of all students, introducing me to so many educators and opportunities over the past three years.

This book could not have happened without the hard work and perseverance of our editor Denise Buschmann who spent hours with Michael and me working through each chapter. Wyatt-MacKenzie Publishing created a publishing process for us that was flawless and so enjoyable. Thank you Nancy Cleary and the entire publishing staff at Wyatt-MacKenzie for your on-going excitement, direction and support beginning with our initial conversation to the final moments of proofing and editing this story.

I am so humbled by all students and parents who literally show up each day sharing their hopes, stories, frustrations, and vulnerabilities with a living school system that has its holes, weaknesses, strengths and possibilities.

Michael, Andrew , Sarah and Regan Desautels, thank you for deeply understanding how this teaching and learning process is such a significant part of my DNA that sometimes I do not share in the excitement of vacations, weekends, and holidays! I love you all so much!

# MICHAEL'S ACKNOWLEDGEMENTS

As human beings, we walk in the direction of our questions. I have been following my questions concerning schooling and education for well over three decades, yet, never would have written a book.

My part of writing this book simply would not have happened if I had not somehow bumped into, my now co-author and friend, Dr. Lori Desautels from Marian University in Indianapolis, Indiana. Lori, thank you for choosing me to co-author *Unwritten, The Story of a Living System*. Without your contagious inspiration it would not have happened. Our collaboration has grown me in many ways and sharing the writing of this book with you has been a joy.

I want to thank all the students that I have shared classroom space with over the years. They have taught me many important lessons concerning what matters most in their schools and classrooms. I am hopeful this work allows what they taught me to be shared and passed along to future teachers.

In addition I would like to thank all the professional educators that I have had a chance to work with over the years. These teachers and school administrators have taught me many fine lessons on what is at the heart of a true education. I have never failed to learn something positive walking around the many schools and classrooms my work has taken me to. It is always a privilege and honor to watch a masterful teacher lead a classroom of young people.

I have also been professionally blessed to have had the opportunity to work with many fine mentors over the years. Dr. Nicholas Long, Professor Emeritus American University and current President of the Life Space Crisis Intervention Institute, as well as co-author of Conflict in the Classroom, has influenced my life in many ways that go well beyond teaching and learning. Dr. Larry Brendtro, the founder of Reclaiming Youth International and author of many fine books concerning young people "at risk" influenced my thinking concerning what is underneath the surface behavior of troubled youth and opened my eyes to really seeing "pain based" behavior.

Much gratitude goes to our editor Denise Bushmann who was a pleasure to work with and to Wyatt-MacKenzie Publishing for choosing to partner with Lori and I and make this book a reality.

A heartfelt thank you to Joan who long ago decided to do this life journey with me. She has supported me through the decades and always made it easy for me to pursue my passion for learning and teaching. Thank you goes to Nate and Maya for confirming to me how human beings unfold and develop and for showing me how deeply humans can love.

# INDEX

# CONTACT THE AUTHORS

Lori Desautels
ldesautels@marian.edu

Michael McKnight
Mcknightmichael816@gmail.com

CPSIA information can be obtained
at www.ICGtesting.com
Printed in the USA
BVHW041145070220
571758BV00009B/109